*Letters For Logan*

# Letters For Logan

A Legacy in Letters of the Determination,
Drive and Heart of Capt. Derek Argel

Deb Argel-Bastian

authorHOUSE

AuthorHouse™
1663 Liberty Drive
Bloomington, IN 47403
www.authorhouse.com
Phone: 1-800-839-8640

© 2012 by Deb Argel-Bastian. All rights reserved.

No part of this book may be reproduced, stored in a retrieval system, or transmitted by any means without the written permission of the author.

Published by AuthorHouse    06/04/2012

ISBN: 978-1-4772-1329-2 (sc)
ISBN: 978-1-4772-1328-5 (hc)
ISBN: 978-1-4772-1327-8 (e)

Library of Congress Control Number: 2012909898

Any people depicted in stock imagery provided by Thinkstock are models, and such images are being used for illustrative purposes only.
Certain stock imagery © Thinkstock.

Because of the dynamic nature of the Internet, any web addresses or links contained in this book may have changed since publication and may no longer be valid. The views expressed in this work are solely those of the author and do not necessarily reflect the views of the publisher, and the publisher hereby disclaims any responsibility for them.

# Prelude Ty's Tribute

In remembering Derek, it is very important that those of us who knew him and loved him not to dwell on the circumstances surrounding his untimely passage. He would not like that. Derek was not one of those timid souls, meekly and cautiously picking his way through life. He was devouring life. Living completely, fully, wasting no time and taking nothing for granted. He got more out of life in the short time he was with us than most people could fit into ten lifetimes. That is how he would like to be remembered.

He was a commanding presence. Strong, fast, a superbly gifted athlete, these were the qualities that would first draw attention to him. These traits he combined with a keen and disciplined mind. He made every endeavor he set his mind to look easy. Nothing seemed to challenge him. He understood, intrinsically, that individuals blessed with such gifts were also burdened with the responsibility to use them for the good of others.

He was warm and engaging, strong but caring, competitive but compassionate, imposing but tender. You were drawn to him, you wanted to follow him; and you knew, somehow, that if you did, everything would be all right.

He was also a lot of fun. Derek could not sit still. He could not be sedentary. There was just too much to do. His life was constant motion. He was out on the water with a fishing pole in his hand or a scuba tank on his back. Gently touching down on the drop zone and then turning around to gather in his parachute. Riding the waves or leading his team on the live-fire range. And always with that warm and engaging smile just waiting to emerge. His life was full and exciting. He was a great friend and companion. The world is a less colorful place without him.

To Wendy, Logan, his family and friends, Derek's life serves as an example of how to live. Take nothing and no one for granted, take advantage of every minute of every day. This is how he must, and will be remembered. FIRST THERE (by Ty, for Derek's memorial)

# Foreword

"Letters for Logan" is a unique tribute to a young man who loved life, his country, and above all, his family and friends.

By all accounts, he was a man with a big heart.

Although I never met Capt. Derek Argel, I've spent time with his family and friends. Through them, I have learned about the man they loved. In addition to being an Air Force Captain, Derek Argel was a brother, a son, a husband, and a father.

On that fateful Memorial Day in 2005 when Derek and his team were killed in Iraq, the lives of their loved ones were forever changed, including his wife, Wendy, and their 10-month old son Logan, who was too young to understand that his father would not be returning.

What started as a letter from a grieving grandmother to her grandson has turned into a memorable tribute to a fallen hero.

When I met Deb a few years ago, she said she wanted to help raise funds for the Special Operations Warrior Foundation and its program to provide college educations to the children of fallen special operators. She started as a volunteer and even participated in a motorcycle ride across the country to raise funds not just for Logan, but for all of the little warriors.

But the most exciting idea was creating this book, this collection of letters for her grandson. Deb had found a perfect way to make sure her son would not be forgotten and that her grandson, and all who read this will know what a special person we have lost.

Logan doesn't have to wonder when he sees someone in uniform, "Did you know my dad?"

Deb, thank you for sharing these stories. You should have no doubt that your courage will help others.

> Edie Rosenthal Lt. Cmdr., U.S. Navy (Ret), Public Relations Director, Special Operations Warrior Foundation

# To the Reader,

It would certainly have been more appropriate for me to call myself the Narrator of this book. In the true sense of the word, I am not the author. The good men and women that have shared their stories for my grandson are the ones who made this book possible. I have attempted to thread the stories together that were written at different times over the past seven years. The characters in this book are real. The main character and subject of the book is my youngest son. Seven years ago, I made a promise that this book would be written and some of his stories would be told. Derek was killed on Memorial Day of 2005, in Iraq. The mission remains classified.

It has been a struggle to make progress on the book, having started it several times only to be shelved. I'm not a writer and I wanted to do justice to my son's memory. I wanted it to be perfect. Finally, I came to the realization that it was time to continue and that the imperfections would be understood. In the writing, I shift many times from speaking to Logan, and back to the reader. Some of the letters overlap in time and may not be in a particular order. Some of the letters are addressed to me, as Logan was too young to receive them at the time.

In the June 4, 2007 edition of *People* Magazine an article appeared called, "Dear Logan, Your Dad was a Hero." It was a story about the idea of this book and the love and testimony of family and friends.

Our family wishes to thank each and every person that contributed to the letters, and those that have helped guide us back to our path. This book is dedicated to every one of you, especially my sons Johnny and Derek, Logan, all of my grandchildren, and those that serve "At the Tip of the Spear."

*Deb Argel-Bastian*

We miss Derek each and every day, but he is still here with us in our hearts. Through him, we have been blessed with new family and friends and the vision of God's greater plan.

Thank you, Deb (Logan's Oma)

# One

Dear Logan,

It has been said that when we are adults, we will be able to count our true friends on one hand. This was not the case with your father. In fact, I can't begin to count the people that he was proud to call his friends. He knew he could count on them, and they could count on him. He listened intently to people and to what they were saying. He cared when he listened. He took the time for his friends and family. He earned their respect, and they earned his. His word and his handshake were his contract, and to his friends a binding and understanding relationship. His departure from this earth to heaven had a step effect that I could never imagine. Some of the friends that wrote these letters, he trusted his life to. They trusted their lives to him.

It would be impossible to include all of the letters, notes and stories we received about him. There are hundreds. This book can only offer a short glimpse or a snapshot into his life and those he touched. In fact, when you read some of these you will understand that he is still touching our lives and has made a difference in the lives of so many.

*These letters really began with two people. Your Dad's lifelong friend had already begun a web page on Memorial Day of 2005. People were able to share their thoughts and some letters on that page. At the memorial service in Florida, your uncle (Big John) had three envelopes containing letters. There was one for me, one for your mother and one for you.*

*If I could tell you just one special thing about your dad, it would be that he was wise beyond his years. If he was sick, he would not take anything for the pain. He said he should experience that pain and know what it was like. He didn't want to take even that moment from his life. He said he wanted to know both pain and joy and that would help make him who he was to become. I didn't know what that meant then, but I know now.*

*The greatest gift that your Dad's friends could have given are these stories. They of course belong to you. You will get all of them just as they were written when it is time. In this book, I have only used call names of your Dad's team mates, or first names only.*

*Because there are so many children that have lost their parents to the recent wars, we hope it will be helpful to other parents, children, friends, relatives. Hopefully, sharing the story of your Dad, will encourage others to write down memories of their own for other families who have lost a loved one. Your dad would want that if it would help in any way. He would be forever thankful to those that took the time to write them to you. I can only share with you how I felt and feel about the loss of my son here on the earth. I can't speak to, or compare anyone else's loss or the impact your Dad had on their lives. This is the beauty of those stories that are shared. These are the stories that bring joy and comfort to us.*

*In this book you will be able to see part of the journey of your Dad's struggles and achievements to attain his personal and military goals.*

*I hope in some way that sharing these memories brings the joy of his life to many, the strength of your mother to all, and the comfort of knowing that your Dad loved you and all that he called friends.*

*Thank you for sharing your stories Logan.*
*Love, Oma May 30, 2012*

It was a beautiful morning. It so happened that the "holiday" of Memorial Day this year just happened to fall on the real Memorial Day. The date was and always will be to our family, the real day. It was also the actual Memorial Day, May 30 that Derek graduated in 2001 from the Air Force Academy. Congress changed the observance day to allow for a three day holiday, a long weekend for people to enjoy picnics, beach trips and other activities. The meaning of the day had become overshadowed over the years. Derek always wanted to attend the services at the Lompoc cemetery and help do his part by putting the flags out. He said, "It was the right thing to do."

We didn't attend the services that morning. In Santa Barbara your grandfather Todd's family was having a breakfast get together, followed by a trip to the Santa Barbara Mission for the Italian Chalk Festival. I charged my phone the night before, hoping I might hear from Derek as it was Memorial Day. He had emailed me a few days before just to say he would be out of touch for some time. At the festival, I stood in awe for some time looking at a beautifully detailed American flag and complimented the artist. For some reason, my eyes began to blur and tear up. I thought of Derek and so many that were away today and so far from home and away from these colors they loved and fought for. I asked Todd if we could leave and go visit his dad. Todd and his dad Hobart, routinely enjoyed cigars and martinis by the pool, and our conversations there were lively, covering all topics. It was peaceful and happy as usual. One hour later, our lives would change forever.

In Ft. Walton Beach, Florida, your mother was out doing a few errands. She had just finished typing an email to your Dad. At the top she wrote, "Memorial Day." Your grandmother Jane was at the house with you, when The Air Force personnel came to the door. Jane called your mother and asked her to come back home right away. Because your grandfather Mike was a retired

Air Force Colonel, they both knew in their hearts this was not a social call.

Sitting at the pool in Santa Barbara, I had chosen the chair nearest the back door at the patio. For some reason, to this day I always choose that chair. My cell phone rang. Sarcastically, I answered, "Happy Memorial Day." It was in bad taste and I knew it. I wanted to withdraw the words as soon as I said them. Derek and I always found the "Happy Memorial Day" signs at local businesses in very poor taste. It was a further reminder that people had forgotten the meaning of that day. I heard your mother's voice on the other end. I was surprised and thought she might be calling to tell me Derek was on the way home or already there. Her voice was steady on the other end. I will never forget the conversation. As Todd and Hobart were engaged in conversation, I put my finger over my free ear to clearly listen to her voice.

"Are you ready for this?", she asked. "Derek's plane has gone down in Iraq." She said she didn't know much more than that they had the site surrounded, and they were looking for someone else. She said they were waiting for confirmation, and she would call me back in about 30 minutes. She told me there were five aboard a small Iraqi plane. In my confusion, I told her that didn't make any sense. What was Derek doing in Iraq? Why was he on an Iraqi plane? Who had the site surrounded?

I hung up the phone and waited for what seemed like an eternity for the call back. I explained to Hobart and Todd what had happened. I asked for another martini while I waited, and even though I was wearing a patch to quit smoking, I asked for cigarettes. Both men tried their best to keep me calm. They said Derek was trained for these things, that he must have jumped or something. My worst thoughts were whispered out loud, "They are not looking for anyone living, these guys don't leave each other."

The phone rang again and your mother said in a soft voice, "It is confirmed." I replied "NO, Wendy." As I tried to get up, I collapsed. Todd caught me and I went into the house to sit down. I remember repeating those words to your mother maybe 20 times. I went back outside to my seat by the pool. I remember Todd telling me that I didn't look well. He told me to move into the shade, that I had too much sun. I didn't feel the sun. The sun was down for me. I would not see daylight again for a very long time.

Suddenly Todd's stepmother Anke was home. She was holding me. Hobart must have called her. She is a caregiver and consoled all of us. I remember saying that we needed to get the earliest flight in the morning to be with Wendy and Logan in Florida. We would need to take my mother. I didn't want her to be at home to answer the door and the endless calls from reporters that would come when the Department of Defense released the information. Anke made all of the arrangements. I managed to make three calls. The first was to my friend Sherry. She was watching a baseball game at a friend's house. I'm sure I didn't make any sense when I asked her to take care of our cat McDuff for the next few days. It seemed she needed no further explanation as I later learned that she saw a ticker come across the screen during the game. It announced that some Air Force Commandos plane had gone down in Iraq. She and her husband Randy were on their way.

The next calls were to my work and to your Aunt Joelle. I told her I could not take care of your cousin, little Derek for the next week. Anke drove Todd and I to tell Uncle Johnny the news. He did not break down in front of me. None of us chose to believe that this was really happening. On the way back to Lompoc, I called the home of Derek's high school water polo coach Bob Lawrence. He was not home, but I explained to his wife Diane that I did not want them to hear it first from the news. I asked them to call everyone as I would be on my way to Florida in the morning. My mother didn't answer the phone. She was still at a barbecue in Ventura. We stopped and left a note on my sister's door to come to my house immediately when they returned and to bring my mother. With them seated on my couch, I had to deliver the news that I didn't want to believe myself. Todd must have made some calls himself, as our friends began to arrive that night. He lit a bonfire in the fire-pit in front of our house and asked that it not go out. The fire-pit was a trademark of our home and the center of so many happy occasions and parties. Your parents, friends and family gathered around it for their wedding rehearsal dinner, and your father burned the last Yule log in it on what would be his last Christmas here on earth.

Sherry, Randy and our friends Joe and Sally had the keys to the house. They agreed to take care of things for us while we were gone for a week. I took a look around the house alone before I packed. The life-size Blues Brothers statues that Derek loved stood their quiet vigil in the dining room as they had in happy times. I went to the back room to touch the buttons on the pinball machine that he set the record on. Desperately, I wanted to go back in time. I wanted to be anyone but me. I wanted to get to Florida to hold you and tell you that things would be all right someday. I wanted to be with you and your mother, part of Derek.

I stared at the fire and the stars that night. I looked to the sky and asked, "Where are you Derek?" We always talked about the stars. As a little boy, he would often ask me if the stars looked the same from everywhere in the world. I told him that I didn't know, but we would find out someday together.

After sobbing into my pillow and praying for some answers, I fell asleep at about 3 a.m. I had a dream. It was March 11, 1977. I was in the delivery room. After a long labor, they laid Derek on my chest. He was a chubby beautiful baby boy. I was laughing that his cry and cooing seemed so deep. I smiled up at the nurse and said, "He is so healthy, and I am so blessed." I closed my eyes and held him close to me. Johnny would have the baby brother he wished for. I knew it would be a boy. Suddenly, the nurse was waking me up to tell me that they had to take him from me to give him a bath and that I would have him back soon. I woke from this dream to my mother's voice gently telling me it was time to go to the airport.

My mother and Todd provided the strength for me to get on the plane in Santa Barbara. I didn't want to board. Somehow, if I didn't get on the plane the nightmare would not be real. I had to be helped, almost carried on board. The flight attendant sat me up front across from her. She held my hand, got tissues and drinks for me. I'll never forget her kindness. In Los Angeles, someone had determined we would miss our flight. They took us off the plane first and down a ramp into a van. We drove at a very high speed across the tarmac and were led on a plane bound for Florida.

Coming down the escalator at the Ft. Walton Beach airport, your grandmother Jane stood alone to meet us. She was strong and kind, but her face was wrenched with pain for all of our loss. Your grandfather Mike was on his way home. As a Delta pilot, he was on one of his work schedules that called him out for several days at a time. He was scheduled to fly when he got the news. They cancelled his flight schedule and got him on the quickest flights home.

I don't know why I thought the house would be quiet when we arrived. I thought we would have some time alone with you and your mother. The house was full of friends, Derek's Air Force brothers and people bringing an endless supply of food. Derek's team was still deployed, but some of the wives and their children were there. Cell phones were ringing all the time and the situation seemed like chaos to me. My phone began to ring constantly and I asked that someone else answer it. I had lots of questions and I needed answers. Valerie Chapman was there. She lost her husband, John "Chappy" Chapman, a Combat Controller, in March of 2002 at the battle of Takur Ghar in Afghanistan. She was there for us as were so many. It soon came to me that each and every person in the room and those calling, had suffered the loss too. We were all gathered together to make some sense of the unthinkable situation.

A long table was set up in the backyard that night. I didn't want to eat, but someone brought me a plate. Your high chair was next to me. My first laugh of the evening was that your mother caught me feeding you all of my mashed potatoes. You loved them, but she wasn't happy with me. I took a glass of wine to the front yard and sat on the tailgate of your dad's truck alone. I looked up at the stars and said out loud, "Where are you Derek?" A calming voice came out of the darkness and said, "He is with me now." I looked around for the source of the voice, but I was physically alone. At that moment, I knew a new journey was beginning for me. I would have to learn to walk again, but I was not alone.

On June 3rd, when the house quieted down a little, your mother suggested we send something to Derek's teammate and friend Ramses via email. We wanted him to read the notes to the others to let them know we were thinking about them as they were still deployed. Your mother went into her walk in closet to write down some of her thoughts in quiet. For a long time, she sat amongst Derek's clothing and penned a comforting letter that told Derek's brothers we were thinking of them and that he would want them to press on.

*To the guys,*

*Wow, where do I start. I never thought I would be writing a letter like this one. I feel like I have so much to say but it is hard to find the words to fit what my heart is telling me. As I am writing this*

*I am sitting in mine and Derek's closet amongst his shoes (yes, it's hard to find room with all of his big shoes around!), his clothes, and everything that reminds me of him. I have by me a pile of emails from Derek, a picture of him, and the Bronze Star that was awarded to him.*

*The memorial was today and it was truly remarkable. You should have seen the support that was there. As we were being driven from the squadron to the hanger, there was a sea of red Berets, your fellow comrades. It was an amazing site to see and I know you would have been proud, I sure was. Of course I know that none of you could be there physically but your hearts were there sitting with me, the other families, and your fellow soldiers.*

*Well, I wanted to write to you and let you know from my point of view what you, as my husband's comrades, meant to him. It is only through his strength that I can write this letter and he is probably looking over my shoulder right now making sure I spell correctly (so if I misspell something you can take it up with him!) Being Derek's wife I have had many conversations with him about all of you and his career field. It is important for me to let you know the love he shared for each one of you and for his country.*

*My husband loved being a combat controller more than anything. I'm sure most of you knew the frustrations that he had when it came to wanting to operate. He expressed to me how he wanted to be able to contribute the way that he felt God intended him to. It was his drive, it was what he was all about. He wanted to be right beside each of you and he wanted to be in the fight. He would have died for any of you and this is something he explained to me before, even though he knew it was hard for me to hear. For the past while, as some of you know, Derek was struggling with a decision-stay in or get out.*

We have had so many emails and phone calls about the pros and cons of both. The reason this decision was so hard for him was because of you, the men he worked beside. I want you to know he wanted to be the one that was there for you guys. He shared blood, sweat, and tears with you and he wanted to see you through to the end. You were his brothers, his family. The Friday before he died, I talked with him and he said, "Baby, I have been sitting on these papers for a week, something is holding me back from signing them." We shared thoughts from the heart and came to the conclusion to stay in the military. I could tell Derek was smiling and at peace with the decision, he was going to continue working beside his brothers.

Respect is something earned by Derek and to each of you he held the highest. As for me, I couldn't be more proud of Derek and all of you that are serving our country. I do not feel anger for losing my husband but proud to call him my husband and proud that he picked me for his wife. I am honored to be associated with such brave men and I want you to continue kicking ass over there. My heart and prayers are with you because I know that I am not the only one hurting over Derek. I look forward to your safe arrival home and hearing any stories you have about my husband that I can share with his son someday. A big Thank You for your friendship to my husband and for making him so proud. Derek has been my hero since the day I met him and what better role model for my son. Logan is the spitting image of his father and he will grow to know what a great man his dad was.

Thank you for the contribution you are making to our country. My husband often used the words "Good Dude" when referring to someone he respected—this was one of his highest compliments. Just know that from this wife's heart that you are all "Good Dudes." Thank you . . . . Wendy

There is no doubt that your mother held it together for the rest of us during this time. Although people kept telling me how strong I was, I felt very weak. I searched for understanding and answers. Honor and Respect were everything to your Dad. He put his heart into everything he did. I remembered back to the third grade, when he came to me enthusiastically and said, "Ma, I know what honor is!" When I questioned him he said, "Honor is your word, it is your promise, and your word always has to be good."

He was always good to his word and did not lightly make a promise. He vowed in the fifth grade, and made a promise to himself that he would enter a military academy and become the best officer and leader he could. God, Country and Family was the code he lived by. When he graduated from the Air Force Academy on Memorial Day of 2001, his quote was "It is above you; to serve God and Country is not a right, but a privilege." On the morning of Memorial Day 2005, before we left for Santa Barbara I remember checking the calendar. It was a Spirit of Freedom calendar. For the month of May the quote was from President John F. Kennedy,

> "Let every nation know, whether it wishes us well or ill, that we will pay any price, bear any burden, meet any hardship, support any friend, oppose any foe, in order to assure the survival and the success of Liberty."

It was one of your father's favorite quotes. When we returned home that evening after receiving the news, I saw the quote again with a much different view. My son had just paid the price as so many before him.

I looked at the computer screen in your mom's home office in Florida and asked Wendy, "Who is the man on your screensaver?" She gently replied, "That is your son." It is the first time that I had seen Derek with a beard and longer hair. It was a picture from his last deployment.

At about 2 a.m. on Wednesday morning, I tried to go up to sleep. I discovered that the large bag I packed to bring to Florida contained only one pair of jeans, Ugg boots, two t-shirts and one pair of sweat pants. When the stores opened that day, I had to shop for something to wear to the memorial for Jeremy, Derek, Brian and Casey at Hurlburt. I explained to the sales woman what I needed and why. She led me to a rack of black clothing. She looked surprised when I said I was not looking for black, but something bright blue. "My son was Air Force," I snapped. I wore the same suit to the service in Lompoc, California, only one week later.

Your dad often used an old military metaphor in all of his training and throughout his life. When I would question him about training or something he was pushing himself to the brink for, he would answer, "It's another tool in my belt ma!" In the days, months and years to follow, I would come to use the suitcase I packed for the trip to Florida on June 1st of 2005 as my own metaphor. I have often packed and unpacked it in my mind, adding the "tools" I would need for this journey. As I was asked to speak about your father at different events, the suitcase became lighter. I had a purpose. The purpose was to tell and share his story and his life.

On June 3rd 2005, a Memorial Service was held for your Dad, Captain Derek M. Argel, Major William "Brian" Downs, Staff Sergeant Casey J. Crate, and Captain Jeremy J. Fresques. This would be our first meeting with the other families. Linda Crate could not make the trip to Florida, but we would meet later at the Arlington service. The hanger was full and I was amazed at the size of the crowd and outpouring of support and love when our families were escorted in. It was just before the service that your uncle "Big John" handed me a letter. He had written three. There was an envelope for your mother, one for you and one for me. Mine read:

*Mrs. Bastian,*

*I wish I could write this letter to you under much different circumstances I too am a parent of two girls. I cannot imagine the pain and loss you are going through. Me being a parent is the first part of why I write this to you. The other part is as Derek's friend, mentor, teammate and soldier. The following is a glimpse of an American hero and the impact he had on my life and those he came in contact with.*

*I met a young, lieutenant named Derek M. Argel, almost more than three years ago. He was very motivated and wanted the world all at once. I can say he reminded me of myself when I was his age. I soon found out what I am sure you already knew, how stubborn he can be. Again, he was so much like the old Sgt who writes this.*

*Derek was the Team Leader. He was carrying much responsibility and getting a limited amount of help from the others on the team. That made me second in command and his Team Sgt. My job is getting anything and everything accomplished on the team. Second to that is training the Team Leader how to lead. After that was making sure the Team Leader was successful in his transition from a young, inexperienced lieutenant into a well-rounded officer. Let's just say he and I butted heads more than once. Derek being hard headed and me being more hard headed. It looks like a bad combination on paper. The reality of it was we had so much in common. This friction is very important in the recounting of my time with him, for this reason. In leadership the ability to put aside emotions, personal differences, take direction and lead has been the downfall or success of many men. Derek asked for help on things he did not know how to attack and accomplish. There was no ego, no resentment and no attitude. He just wanted to be a better leader for his men. Derek would make any sacrifice to make that happen.*

*We talked about our lives, the good, the bad and ways we could save the world. In those conversations I learned the respect and love he had for his mother. He proudly told me the sacrifices you made to give him and his brother a better life. I don't think I have ever heard anyone speak so highly of his mother. I asked him about the tattoo on his back. He told me it was about you. "Never forget" it says. People that really knew Derek know this love made him the man, friend, husband, father and leader he became. That is a testament to you. These talks reminded me of my mother who did the same by herself. One more thing we could share and bring us closer as friends. Some might say we crossed the line of the professional relationship. I say we did not. We bonded as men and as brothers. You have to do that in this job.*

*During this time we trained all over the country. We were away from our loved ones and spent more time with each other than them. We became family. I explained earlier what my job was as Team Sgt. That is important to understand. I was in a position, much like a father or mother. Derek grew as a man and leader. The reward is watching someone grow into the person he wants to be. I was fortunate to be a witness of his growth into a professional soldier. He constantly worked on making himself better. He attacked problems. Some his own, most of them were someone else's. Regardless, he found solutions.*

*The young kid I was mentoring ended up saving me from myself. There was a time in my life where my judgment failed me miserably. Derek stood in front of the commander and convinced him that I was worth more than the problem that was before him. He kept me from getting in any recourse, saving my career.*

*His focus and motivation kept me from quitting on myself at scuba school. We were swim buddies. The instructor staff at the school called us "Team America." The reason is because we were so fast. Truth of it is I had to swim for my life not to be drowned by Derek. We had one more 3,000 meter swim to do and we had never been beat. I was physically and mentally exhausted. Derek saw more in me than I could see in myself. He said to me, "John, just one more time. Give me one more." He knew I would regret it the rest of my life if I did not suck it up and do it. He was right. When it was all said and done, we destroyed everyone.*

*In my fifteen years of service, I have never had more respect for an officer than I have for Captain Derek M. Argel. He showed me that he cared deeply for his men. He believed with every fiber of his body that what he was doing was right. He took personal responsibility in holding everyone to a higher standard, including himself. Never sacrificing his integrity for anyone, anytime or any place. By his leadership, friendship and example I am a better man today.*

*Know that your son did not die without purpose. He is the standard for the Special Operations community. Captain Argel's example will make all of the community to train harder, lead more effectively, be more responsible for their actions and the actions of their men.*

*Many leaders in Derek's position hide behind a desk and remain there for their career. Your son was not that type of leader. On Memorial Day, he led from the front, operating and leading his men in a combat. Giving up everything he had or was going to, for something bigger than himself . . . us. I would have followed Derek into Iraq, that Monday, May 30, 2005. Knowing the outcome, I would have still followed him. Without a doubt. Why? His leadership, friendship commanded loyalty and respect.*

*I would like to thank you on behalf of my family, the men that are here and those that cannot be, for your son's devotion to duty to his men and country. My life and the men that served with him, that were led by him, are better today because of it.*

*He will be missed. He will be remembered as what he sacrificed to be. An operator and leader of warriors. Your son epitomizes the code all Special Tactics Combat Controllers and Pararescuemen live by: "First There, That Others May Live." Big John, June 2005*

I treasure this letter just as I have since the day I received it. I would see John and thank him again just one week later in Lompoc. I had no real concept of time then and each minute, each day seemed the same. Time just seemed to stop. We flew home from Florida just three days before the service that was being planned at home. Your Godfather K (Kelii) was on his way from Korea. Your Dad's friend Charlie was coming in from Italy and many others from a great distance.

While I was in Florida, Sherry was planning the service here in Lompoc on June 10th. We talked several times a day 3,000 miles apart. I remember that she tried to convince me that we should hold the reception at a large hall following the service at the cemetery. I told her I wanted to have it at my home. I didn't think we would have that many attend due to the short notice. I was not able to acknowledge what happened. Only days before, our friends Gil and Vicki tragically lost their daughter. I thought of them and what they were going through. Clearly, during this time everyone else was thinking for me.

When we arrived home from Florida the bonfire was still burning. Our friends had manned it 24/7 since Memorial Day. Our friend Ross owns a tree service and he brought load after load of wood to keep it going. Our house was clean inside and out. While we were gone, teams of friends detailed our back yard and every part of the service to take place. Derek's water polo coaches Bob Lawrence and Bob Boyer made all of the arrangements for the Cabrillo portion of the service along with lifetime friend Dave Riley. I began to panic a little, but we were in good and loving hands. Everyone wanted to help do something in Derek's honor. Our good Mayor Dick DeWees worked with Sherry. Our entire street was blocked from traffic on both ends. City buses were arranged to bring people from the local shopping center to our home. Vandenberg Air Force set up a long row of tents in the street to accommodate everyone. Our service organizations and BBQ teams pitched in together and cooked Derek's favorite BBQ tri-tip and chicken for 1,000 people. Our new neighbors had just moved in, but offered to let us put up a tent for memorabilia and pictures. The entire city of Lompoc came out larger than life to honor Derek and pay their respects. With Kelii, the Pentagon approved an F-16 flyover and missing man formation. Later in the back yard with my friends I confessed to Sherry, "Well, you were right about the large crowd." We were so honored and blessed that your Dad made such an impact in the lives of so many. Grandma and Grandpa Jane and Mike, your Mom and you were here as well as so many from the Academy, high school, and the Combat Control family.

# Two

One of the greatest influences on Derek's young life was his close relationship with my mother. My father died when Derek was very young, but Derek remembered him well. My mother, who everyone calls Momo, shares some of her early memories.

> To Logan: "A Grandmother Remembers"
>
> *How well I remember the first time I saw Derek—the big husky baby boy with the round face, and the little crooked smile. He was always happy with a deep belly laugh. As he grew, he was like a sturdy block. I remember how upset we both were when he became too heavy for me to lift.*
>
> *Beginning with pre-school, he was very serious about learning. When it was time to go home at the end of his pre-school day, he would have to go back and check his "cubby" one more time.*
>
> *Derek loved elementary school and his teachers adored him because he had such an inquisitive mind and worked hard.*
>
> *I remember his first team sport was youth soccer (maybe when he was in about the first or second grade); and the coach put*

him in as goalie. Well, the game got underway; and the ball was headed for Derek's goal. Imagine our concern when we looked down that way, and Derek was completely wrapped up in the net like a mummy. Later he told us that he didn't like to play "goldie." He continued to play soccer, wrestled, played Little League, joined in martial arts, and started early in age-level swimming classes. He played a little basketball, but it just wasn't his sport.

Logan, your Dad always loved wild life of all sorts. He collected lizards, snakes, bugs—you name it! Our next door neighbor kept a bench in the backyard. Derek would move that bench over by her terrace so he could climb up and look for lizards. She finally just left the bench in place, so it was handy for him. It's still there.

Derek had lots of friends in Middle School, including his buddy and younger cousin Clint. They enjoyed many projects together—one that I remember very well was their attempt to build an airplane in my back yard. They found some scrap lumber and some of Dado's old nails. Derek took the motor out of his mother's lawn mower. They worked several days, reassuring me that the plane would really fly, and when they got it out of the yard, they would clean up the mess.

As he was growing up, Derek didn't like girls much but he was willing to help them. Once, I remember when he was on a youth basketball team, he had a girl on his team who never got a basket. Once, they were near the basket at the same time and there was no defense near. He gave her the ball and let her make the shot.

It was in Middle School that Derek was introduced to computers and computer games. He had a neighborhood friend and classmate and they spent many hours on the computer doing competitive games and problem solving. It was during that period *of time that the two boys were able to go to a NASA Space Camp in Huntsville, Alabama. Derek had a great time.*

*It was in early elementary school that his love of fishing began. He had no equipment; but he really didn't need it. He and his cousin would stand on a pier for hours with baited strings in the water, trying to catch crabs. Even though I was their transportation for some of these excursions, I don't believe I ever remember seeing any crabs, but I'm sure they probably threw them back.*

*When Derek was 10 or 11, his mother and I were fortunate enough to be able to take the children on some nice family trips. We took an auto tour of most of the historical places on the upper East Coast. Derek absorbed it all like a sponge. He loved Washington, D.C., the Statue of Liberty, and many other sites; but I think his favorite spot was the top of Mt. Washington in New Hampshire. On brother Johnny's 12th birthday, their mom and I took them on their first trip to Honolulu, where they enjoyed surfing lessons.*

*About midway through elementary school, Derek, his brother John, and his cousins Serena and Clint, joined an age-level swimming club called the Lompoc Marlins. After several years of that training, all four became excellent swimmers. This led to a love of water polo. Derek started water polo training the summer before he entered high school. He swam and played water polo all four years of high school. I went to most of the games and swim meets to cheer them on.*

*Logan, your dad's performance was never "good enough" in his opinion. When he finished a swim event, I would go to the end of his lane and compliment him. I'd say, "Good swim, Bub!" He would always answer the same way. "Thanks, but it was NOT a good swim."*

*When he finished high school, he wanted to go to the Naval Academy at Annapolis. His scores were not quite high enough for eligibility; so your Oma sent him to a private prep school in Malibu, California. When he finished there, his scores were higher, but still lacked a few points to be enough for the Academy. Meanwhile, Col. Jeff Heidmous, the water polo coach at the Air Force Academy wanted Derek. After much thought and soul-searching, your Dad decided to accept an appointment to the Air Force Academy prep school, in order to raise his scores to the level they required. There was no guarantee that he would get an appointment to the Academy after prep school. The family traveled to Colorado for his prep school graduation. All of us had sweaty palms and a prayer on our lips that he would get an appointment. His hard work paid off and he was appointed as a cadet to the Academy. He went from academic probation as a Freshman to the Dean's list when he graduated. He was on the water polo team all four years and graduated with honors in athletics.*

*After graduation, your Dad could have stayed on at the Academy with a position in the Athletic Dept.; but he didn't want that. He wanted to be a combat controller, which is one of the most dangerous jobs in the Air Force.*

*The Air Force placed him where he wanted to be; so consequently he was sent to Hurlburt Field in Florida for extensive training.*

*After months of training, he would go back and forth to the Middle East (or somewhere) for a particular mission. When it was completed he would come back to his home base in Florida. It was during one of these "down" times, after an assignment, that he met your mother and fell "head over heels" in love with her.*

*Derek was a brave man who was dedicated to his country, to his job, his comrades and friends. You can always be proud of being his son, as I am his grandmother. Always know that his deepest love was for you and your mother. "Never Forget!" Love, Momo*
*June 2007*

When Derek was still a baby, I accepted a job at the Houston Zoo. My mother and I made the long trip together from California with Johnny and Derek in my little jeep, pulling a trailer with everything I could fit. After a few months in temporary rentals and housing, we settled in Pearland, Texas. At that time, Pearland was still out in the country. I was able to rent a place with 20 acres, a barn and a large pond. The barn allowed us the opportunity to board horses and supplement my income from the zoo. The pond was a blessing for Derek and Johnny. We took our chairs and lunch down there on hot afternoons to just relax sometimes. The boys would cool off in the pond and Derek would fish for whatever he could with his little Zebco fishing pole.

It seems we were always outside with the horses, doing chores and seeing what Derek would collect next. Each time he caught something, he would look it up in one of my books and really examine it before letting it go.

On some weekends that I had to work, the boys would come to the zoo with me. They enjoyed helping to feed and take care of the animals. Derek especially enjoyed the duck lake and feeding meal worms to the ducks and geese. Someone pulled into the zoo one day and brought an unwanted large white goose. Like so many other animals we took in, the goose came home with us. We named her Goose Helen, and she became the best "watch dog" we ever owned. Johnny and Derek never forgot her. As grown men they looked back on that time and teased me that I put their lives in danger with a mean goose.

On weekends that I didn't work, we would make trips to LBJ lake near Austin Texas to fish for bass followed by floating down the river in New Braunfels and more fishing. The three of us were always off on some adventure with friends.

A short time later, I read that Miami was about to open a new zoo. At that time, zoos were mostly places where animals remained in cages and not a more natural environment. The new Miami Zoo would have the motto, "No Herds Barred." I sent in an application and soon the boys and I were off on a new adventure. While I made the move, the boys came home to Lompoc to stay with my parents.

I was able to find a place to rent in Homestead, Florida. It had five acres and was close to the Florida Keys and the Everglades. When the boys came out to join me, we took advantage of all of the activities in the area. We canoed in the Everglades, went shrimping in the Keys and collected snakes and lizards with the reptile folks from the zoo. Derek loved to hold the emerald tree snakes and the smooth indigo snakes. He looked up everything we collected in my books and seemed to memorize the information. He would recite these facts to Johnny and I until we could pass his informal quizzes. I think that is why friends later in life referred to these lessons as "Derek's factoids." He thought that since he had taken the time to learn all of these things, others really should be interested.

As a single divorced mother of two, things became financially more difficult for us. The Miami area was expensive. It was also time to begin thinking about Johnny's elementary school education. The schools in the area catered to many transient families that came to Florida to escape the cold winters in the north. I spoke to my parent's and explained that I would like to move back home. I wanted the boys to go to the elementary school that I attended. They agreed that Johnny and Derek should not attend an underachieving school. My father's health was quickly deteriorating and that also weighed heavily on my mind. My parents had been out to visit us in Texas and we made trips home for holidays and vacations, but it just wasn't the same.

In April, 1983 we moved back to Lompoc and the boys were enrolled in Buena Vista Elementary School. I eventually bought a home just five houses down from my mother and only a few houses away from Cabrillo High School. It wasn't long before we had a constant flow of kids coming in and out, and both Johnny and Derek became involved in sports, scouting, and Sunday School. The surrounding woods became a favorite hiking place for Derek to take up his reptile collecting and building forts with his friends.

I remember having only one discussion about youth football. I had spoken with doctors about head injuries and worse, so the discussion was very short. My answer was no. Soon after, both boys were enrolled in swim lessons and joined the local swim team. The friendships and bonds for parents and swimmers lasted a lifetime. We traveled together on weekends, ate together and cheered all of our swimmers on. One of the great friendships we forged was with the Riley family.

> *Oh how I remember Derek well! He and I were swimmers for the Marlins swim team in Lompoc for many years. If you know anything about swim meets, they are grotesquely long, with huge breaks between events. As kids you must figure out any way to keep yourselves entertained. Derek and I had gone crazy by about 12 noon and started to figure out ways to pass the time; we decided to beat box. Beat boxing is basically making crazy sounds out of our mouths by slobbering all over the place. Over time that too became dull, so we noticed two lines in the concrete pool of the deck. In between the two lines we labeled it as the, "no beats zone." When people walked into the "no beats zone,"*

we stopped beat boxing. Upon strangers exiting the "no beats zone" we started our insidious beats sharing equal measures in our song. We usually said something of the sort when passing the beat to each other, "Now on to my homie Derek Werek and Merik." Without hesitation, Derek started his version of the beat box song.

It sounds silly that after all Derek and I went through together that this is one of my fondest memories. I have never forgotten how he and I could act like complete fools and get away with it . . . well, so we thought!

I remember how Derek, his brother Johnny, and Mother Debbie would talk about how poor they were. Of course, my family up for any challenges the Argel family would put forth, had to challenge them to really see who was the poorer family! In the early 1990's Burger King came out with a new product, the "Burger Buddies." Today you will find these bite sized burgers on appetizer menu's named, "Sliders." We often joked that we had to split a single "Burger Buddy" with our entire family.

One day after swim practice, the doorbell rang. I calmly walked to the door and opened it expecting a visitor. Unfortunately, there was no one there! I looked up, to the right, left, and then down to find a bright shining box of Burger Buddies! I would like to remember that a choir was singing and a single white light was shining on the box, but alas there they were steaming and smelling delicious on my porch. As I picked them up, I heard Derek, Johnny and Debbie trying to hold back their laughter. I looked over the hedge that was in our yard and there was the entire Argel clan . . . snickering and laughing in the bushes in the front of our house! We still reminisce about the Burger Buddies! I recently saw a commercial for those same burgers, only they were named something else. It doesn't matter what they are called now. Sliders will always be, "Burger Buddies" to me.

As we graduated high school and became of age to drink alcohol, we all decided to go to a party. Of course at this time, Derek had not met the love of his life, Wendy, yet and we were going out to meet some girls. Since Derek and I have absolutely no skill in meeting the ladies, we had to get our courage up. So, we went to the local store and picked up some beer. I really don't remember what type of beer I was drinking, but will never forget the flavor Derek chose. We were comparing beer and Derek pulled this huge 40 ounce beer out of his bag and yelled, "Chicks dig the Crazy Horse!" With Derek's goofy smirk, he turned the top of the beer, "This stuff tastes like hell!" His face was classic! Trying to swallow his pride he gave a disgusted look that I can't describe. I think he threw his Crazy Horse away. It didn't matter what the chicks thought about this beer, he was definitely done with this brew.

While others obviously weren't there and probably cannot appreciate my stories, what everyone can say is that Derek was a fantastic friend! I loved him like a brother (as did many others). Derek was always there for each and every one of his friend. He loved his country, family, wife, and beautiful son. I have never met another person with as much integrity as Derek Mears Argel possessed, I'm not sure I will ever meet one again. I have been blessed to have a friend and brother like Derek. I can only imagine how proud Logan must be of who his daddy is, was and always will be. Derek was a miracle to all of us and I am proud to have had him as my friend. With Love and Respect, David Riley March 2012

Coach Bob Lawrence and his wife Diane had two sons. Both Matt and Bret became good friends and teammates of Johnny and Derek.

*Logan,*

*There are a number of memories that I have with Derek, but the one that I think about the most is a time that Tom Rudolfs, John, Derek and I went to Point Magu to surf. We surfed here every time Derek would come home and always had a wonderful time as these trips are still hands down the best surf days I've had. We would stay at my place in Santa Barbara the night before going to Point Magu and it was always like Christmas morning for all of us as we rarely would be able to enter the base unless Derek was in town. We would tease Derek about getting a special salute when we would enter the base, because the gate officer would always stand a bit more erect once they realized his rank. We thought it funny at the time, but all of us had a sense of pride of how well Derek was doing in the Military (Derek would never boast about his successes during his time served, but we knew!)*

*Once we got to the break it was always "going off", but this day had a little extra size to it. We all were having a great time and catching some amazing waves, but Derek had this unbelievable barrel and finished it with an "el rollo" which caught everyone's eye. We would always act like no one saw each other's good waves, but each of us had to give it up to Derek on this one as it was very impressive. After the wave we all were waiting for the next set and John was off to the left and the set wave ended up where he was at, so Derek, Tom and I sat and watched John try to upstage Derek's wave and as John began to paddle into it he was too high on the peak and decided to throw his board and go crashing into the break zone. We all started laughing uncontrollably as this is not what John regularly does. I still laugh at the thought of that scenario as it is still vivid in my mind and I can still hear Derek's loud goofy laugh. We finished the day exhausted sitting on the bed of my truck watching the sunset and not wanting the day to ever end. It has never ended in my mind as I frequent this place in my thoughts often.*

*I hope you are doing well and I know you've heard it a thousand times, but Derek was an amazing guy and had exemplary character! He is missed every day! Matt Lawrence March 2012*

Both your Dad and Uncle Johnny were blessed to have great coaches from age group swimming through college. They provided not only coaching, but lessons in patience, good sportsmanship and ethics. I am forever grateful to all of them for what they provided to my sons. In swimming and water polo throughout the years, we were more like a big family.

*I coached thousands of young men and women in my three decades of aquatics coaching at Cabrillo and no one athlete was any more important to me (except, of course Matt and Bret Lawrence) than Derek and his brother John. I loved Derek like a son, and he unabashedly felt the same way about me. We hugged like father and son, and I was/am as proud of him as I could possibly be. Derek had a knack of making everyone he knew feel as though he/she was his best friend. He loved people and was never ashamed to let his friends know how much he loved them. We, in the Cabrillo water polo family, are a proud group of athletes who are very proud of our traditions and our heritage, but we are especially proud of the accomplishments that we have made after our time at Cabrillo. Our friend, Derek Argel made the ultimate sacrifice, doing exactly what he wanted to be doing. He wanted to fight for his country. He told me a few months ago that he wanted desperately to get the opportunity to do what he was trained to do. He died doing just that. He died for us. Bob Lawrence, Cabrillo High School (June 2005)*

I'm not even sure Derek was in high school yet when he first went to Coach Lawrence and asked permission to lift weights and work out with the team. Derek began to ask me questions all of the time about what he called "gifted or natural" athletes. He questioned why his brother was so much faster. It was true, and really a sight on the deck of the pool so many times. He wondered how it was possible that while he was warming up for a swim with jumping jacks, etc., that his brother could sit back with earphones, not warm up, jump on the block and win the race. He questioned his own ability and started asking his brother for help.

*Dear Logan,*

*Derek was my brother and best friend. He was the best man I ever knew and 6'6" of solid muscle. He could run, swim and if he wanted, could really whip anyone. He wouldn't though, because although he was a "bad ass" he was also the most humble man I knew. There isn't a minute that goes by that I don't think of him, miss him and want him back. I look at you and sometimes hold back the tears. You look and act like him so much in everyday life.*

*When your Dad died, a big part of me went too. Everything in my life fell apart and part of me wanted to give up, but it's not in our blood to ever quit. I live for you, little Derek and our family. I thank God for every second I got to spend with my brother on earth. Real super heroes don't wear capes, they just have big hearts and your Dad had the biggest.*

*Your dad wasn't always the giant you see in pictures. He wasn't always the guy who set records. When your Dad was young he was not strong, or a fast athlete. He was short, a little chubby and pretty slow. He spent a long time trying to live in my shadow, as I was at that time pretty good in sports and a decent athlete. One day when he was still in high school, your Dad came into my room and was extremely upset after a game that he sat on the bench for most of. He said, "How come I'm not as good, as fast, and as strong as you are." I told him that he could be strong, fast and anything he wanted to be if he was willing to work for it. I told him that if everyone else was working out for two hours, then he would have to make it three, and that he would have to work harder than the rest.*

*After that day I watched his transformation from a slow and what I considered a little chubby boy, into a giant driven machine that never slowed down, but only got faster. He may have tried to live in my shadow for a little while when we were younger, but later others would stand in his shadow.*

*Your dad had more heart than anyone I know, or have ever known. I will always love him more than anyone will ever know. I Love You! Uncle Johnny July 2006 "Never Forget"*

Derek tried many sports back to back before he made a decision about what he felt he was really good at and had many disappointments. When he was twelve or thirteen, he tried Karate for about six months. At a tournament we attended, he stood facing the audience with the first place trophy he had been awarded. I could tell by the look on his face that something was wrong. When it was time to leave, he asked me to wait just a minute. He walked up to the boy with the second place trophy and said, "I know what the judges decided, but you and I know who won." The boy's father looked very surprised when Derek said, "I can't leave here without trading trophies with you." He told them to please trust his decision, and that this would be a great favor to him. In the parking lot on the way to the car, he said, "Ma, I don't think Karate is for me anymore."

In high school before swimming started, he tried basketball. I think back that people thought he would be good at it because of his height. It was a very tough decision to make after starting on the team, as he never wanted to let anyone down.

*In Derek's junior year at Cabrillo he tried out for and made the JV basketball team that I coached. Every day at practice was an*

*adventure as he worked hard to get his water polo body to adjust to a land sport. I thought he was making adequate progress and was playing 6-10 minutes a game. This adequate progress wasn't good enough for him as he had excelled at a Varsity sport, and now struggled at this level. We had some post game and post-practice discussions as he dealt with his frustrations. I saw that he had a burning desire to succeed in everything that he undertook. (The path that he took to get into and successfully complete his coursework at the Air Force Academy is a testament to this.) After one particularly frustrating game he came to me with tears in his eyes and said that his performance was adversely affecting the team and he just felt it best if he got started with the swim team a little early. I didn't agree with him but wished him well, thanked him for the contribution that he gave to the team and told him to have a great season in swimming, which he did.
Dan Duffy, Jr. June 2005*

All of Derek's coaches had a profound effect on his life. They contributed to his sense of humor, reminding him not to take himself so seriously all of the time, but to stay focused. Johnny started calling his brother "D" at a very early age for a nickname. It quickly caught on and everyone close to him called him "D." It branched out in high school and at the Academy to other variations. He would often come to the pool deck and proclaim himself something D (eg. "D'elicious D") and always with a smile or entertaining little dance to get things started. Derek felt himself so fortunate to have a water polo coach at the Academy, who had also played at his high school and later for the Academy. I credit Jeff Heidmous for taking Derek under his wing and guiding his success both in the rigors of studies and in the pool.

There were many regulars around our house as the boys were growing up. One of your dad's lifelong friends was Charlotte.

*Dear Logan,*

*Where does one start telling a son about how truly amazing his father is? I'm not sure that written word would do your father justice, but I will do my best.*

*I was blessed to have shared a good portion of my childhood with Derek. From our time at Vandenberg Middle school, to those visits home when we were back for holidays from College, he was always a cheerful presence in my life. French class and water polo games would not have been the same without him! Derek was always kind, super goofy (the best kind of goofy) and an incredibly loyal friend. I can' t say that I have ever heard anyone utter anything but praise and admiration for him. I always admired him for his dedication and persistence.*

*I recall a few conversations with him when he was working to transfer to the Air Force Academy. It was a tough endeavor, but he kept his eye on the prize and never gave up. It surely wasn't easy, but it was worthwhile. All of us beamed with pride when we found out that he had been admitted and that all the hard work paid off! Derek was an incredible man. The goofy sweetheart grew up to be a focused warrior. When I saw him in San Diego and he was looking at the possibility of becoming a Navy Seal, I saw a "new and improved" Derek. It was still Derek, but there was intensity about him that I had not seen before. Perhaps, there were flickers of this intensity when he was crushing the competition in the pool, but nothing as consistent as what I saw in San Diego. He was now a man with purpose.*

*It's really difficult to think of just one story or memory of Derek. Every moment with him was memorable and full of laughter! He was a gentle giant that lit up a room just by being there. I loved his deep bellows-like laugh with an occasional snort. When he laughed, he REALLY laughed, which just made everyone laugh harder. When he smiled he had a big toothy grin that was unbelievably contagious. Looking through photos of you as you get older, I see that same toothy grin in you. I see so much of him in you! Who am I kidding? Every time I see you, I see Derek's "Mini-me!" Ha! I love seeing family photos of you growing up, and know that you have been blessed with an incredible family that loves you so very much.*

*I am looking forward to the day when we all get together during one of our periodic "reunion weekends" so that we can personally share with you laughs and mildly embarrassing stories about your father! Oh that laugh . . . it is something I will never forget. Your Father, is someone we could never forget. He was a great man, Logan, and I am so incredibly blessed to have called him my friend. All my love, and then some . . . Charlotte Hufschmidt, Redondo Beach, CA April 2012*

The Lawrence brothers were regulars in our lives, as well as their parents Bob and Diane. Matt's younger brother Bret wrote the following:

*Derek impacted a lot of people in his life. He was a funny, passionate, loyal friend that everyone admired. However, the one quality that impacted my life the most was Derek's strong work ethic.*

*As a snotty little freshman coming onto the swim team, I did not have the faintest understanding of hard work. Like most other 15 year olds, I went through the motions in practice and did only what was required of me by the coaches. As luck would have it, our Varsity swim team needed a few extra bodies to fill in at meets, specifically someone to fill in for the dreaded 500 yard freestyle event. So, my name was called to make the move up from the JV team and join the big leagues.*

*I started practicing with the Varsity guys and immediately recognized the pace was harder and the intensity was much higher. Guys didn't sit out a set and they didn't loaf on any laps. This was a distinct change from my JV brethren. In fact, if you did take a breather, you'd get the death stare from Derek and his imposing 6'5" frame from the lane next to you (i.e. the fast lane). He didn't have to say anything, but you immediately realized that if he is giving 100% there is no reason why you should not be doing the same.*

*After a few weeks of the silent but forceful peer pressure, I started noticing my performance improving. I also started really enjoying the workouts, competitiveness and the camaraderie. In fact, I stopped thinking about the workouts as a chore and actually couldn't wait to go to practice. There were a number of the guys on the team that year that actually stayed after practice to get extra yards in. In effect, Derek single handedly raised the intensity of our team through the example of the excellence he pursued for himself.*

*For the next few years, I had the privilege of having Derek as a teammate and later the pleasure of having him return as an alumni to help train our team. Throughout those years, Derek always inspired me to push myself beyond my comfort zone. He gave me the confidence to identify goals I wanted to achieve and aggressively attack them with full confidence that I could accomplish whatever I set my mind to. In all honesty, I think our 1996 CIF water polo title had a lot to do with Derek and the foundation he set for us when we were underclassmen.*

*Today, I still have the pamphlet from Derek's memorial service sitting right in front of me at my office. I do this to not only remember Derek, but also to remind myself of the lessons he taught me. In fact, I would say several times a month I am motivated to try a new challenge simply by looking at Derek's picture. In my mind, it's what he would have done.*

*There were a lot of great lessons that Derek would have taught you Logan. He was a great man and his life was purpose-driven. Hopefully some of these memories will help instill in you the wonderful qualities that Derek taught all of us. He is and will always be missed, but his mark will last forever. Bret Lawrence March 2012*

# Three

Derek enjoyed telling folks that he was a "double preppie." He laughed about it, but also used it as a tool, when encouraging other cadets at the Academy. He never hesitated to let the younger cadets know that he really got his start at Northwestern Prep School. It taught him how to endure the rigors of the Academy and what to expect when he got there. He loved the staff and related to others how fortunate he was to have been given a chance there. One of his great and lifetime friends, Brandon Lingle or "BJ" would be attending with him. BJ shares the following memories:

*Dear Logan,*

*Refugio Beach is about a half-hour drive from Lompoc. A rocky point marks the northwest end of the beach which stretches southeast to form a crescent shaped cove. Palm trees line the grass on the edge of the sand to give the beach a tropical feel. On foggy mornings, you can almost sense the pirates that once anchored in the small bay. When the fog clears, oil-rigs are the only obstructions to a pristine view of Santa Rosa Island.*

*During Christmas break in 1996, your Dad and I took a trip down to Refugio. On the drive south Sublime blared from the speakers of my truck while we told stories from our first few months in Colorado Springs. We laughed about our difficulties with classes and the newness of military life. We also remembered growing up in Lompoc and our time at Northwestern Prep School. We were pretty much the only people at the beach that day. It was raining. The clouds made the greenish-blue water appear slate grey. The rain felt warm on our faces compared to the cool Pacific. There wasn't much of a swell, but we had a great time nonetheless.*

*In some ways that trip seems to encapsulate your Dad. To him, the trip was always as much, if not more fun, than the destination itself. Superficial obstacles like no waves or bad weather only added to the adventure. Road trips with your Dad were great. The destination didn't matter—the beach, Santa Barbara, Malibu, Temecula, or Aspen—everyone was sure to enjoy themselves. Derek lived in the moment and made everything fun.*

*Your dad and I were born six days apart in different states. My family didn't move to Lompoc until 1987. That's when I met D. We were 5th graders at Buena Vista Elementary School. Although he didn't have his amazing height then, he stood out in other ways. He was friends with everyone. He made me, the new guy at the time, feel welcome. I remember him running for class president or some other school government thing. I don't remember if he won, but his campaign was successful. It wasn't because he was the only candidate to hand out candy, but because he was the most sincere and genuine guy out there. Even as 5th graders, we could see it. This never changed. He ended his note in my senior yearbook..."Your Pal, Derek"—that epitomizes your Dad...everyone's pal.*

*During high school, he wanted to be a Navy SEAL. He wanted to go to the Naval Academy, and I wanted to go to the Air Force Academy. Neither one of us had the grades or SAT scores to get into either of those schools. We both chose to go to Northwestern (NWP) in hopes of achieving those goals.*

*On a foggy morning in August 1995, your Dad and I drove down the PCH to County Line Beach near Malibu. That's where NWP was at the time. We were so excited because that road trip of several hours was the symbolic start of life after high school—the first tangible step toward our goals. It was our first time away from home for any significant amount of time. Your dad's Beastie Boys CD, Ill Communication, was the main soundtrack for that trip. I'm sure he was wearing one of his Navy SEAL t-shirts. We talked some about the previous summer in Lompoc, but we talked more about the future. We stopped at In-n-Out in Ventura for lunch. That day he introduced me to the 4x4. That massive burger has four patties and four slices of cheese. It isn't even on the menu. You have to ask for it. You dad didn't mess around when it came to eating. Anyway, we weren't hungry when we arrived at the NWP campus. The school was perched on a hillside overlooking the Pacific. The view was incredible. We could see Anacapa Island, Santa Cruz Island and Point Mugu from pretty much anywhere on campus.*

*Since we lived just a few hours from the school, we had volunteered to go early to help set up. After meeting the people who ran the school—Mr. Hoiby and the Durbecks—we helped move the school's stuff from a shed, down a narrow trail, to the school's main building. Derek, me and a few other guys carried Mr. Hoiby's 500 pound podium. This was sort of tricky since the mountain was on one side and a 10-foot drop was on the other. We made it without banging that podium up too bad—I think.*

*We were roommates at NWP. The dorms had three large rooms with a community bathroom in the middle. Six or seven guys lived in each of the rooms. Your dad had to sleep on the top of the only bunk bed because of his height. His feet had to hang over the* edge of the bed. The lower beds wouldn't work because they were enclosed by the big wooden boxes where we hung our clothes. He took his sleep very seriously. Nobody would mess with your Dad when he was asleep. He would throw one of his giant shoes or a fist at any poor fool who did. All of the guys in our room were from California except one who was from Virginia. One of our roommates played Pink Floyd's "Wish You Were Here" and Neil Young's "Heart of Gold" every night. We would go to sleep BS'ing while listening to those songs and the ocean.

On weekdays, we ate all of our meals together in a large room that was also the main classroom. That building was the hub of NWP social life since it had a big screen TV and a pool table. After breakfast, we would learn the finer points of English from Mr. Hoiby. After lunch, Mrs. Durbeck taught math and chemistry. At times Mr. Hoiby could be pretty intense, so Mrs. Durbeck's classes were usually a welcomed change.

The Hoibster made us memorize long lists of vocabulary words. D would always pick out a few of those works and use them repeatedly. I think he did this to annoy us as much as he did it to memorize the words. He especially liked "zephyr"—a gentle breeze.

Mr. Hoiby taught grammar from ancient red textbooks that were issued to us. We all became expert at diagramming sentences and identifying dangling participles. Near the end of the semester we had to pass the dreaded Review 3. It covered everything in that text. Reviews 1 and 2 were terrible, so we knew that Review 3 could be disastrous. Luckily, Derek's book had a kind of treasure map to find a contraband copy of Review 3. The previous year's students had thoughtfully hidden it for us. We spent a few hours in deciphering the clues. We eventually found a completed copy of Review 3 stashed in a plastic bag inside the heater hanging from the ceiling of our room. It seems *that the guys from the previous year spent more time hiding that thing than working on it. We weren't geniuses by any means, but we soon realized that the hidden copy wasn't exactly error free.*

*But NWP wasn't all work. Mr. Hoiby liked to tell stories, and he was good at it. He recounted his days at Annapolis in a way that motivated us all. He also told grand stores of past NWP class antics. He ended class early a few times so we could watch the final days of the OJ Simpson trial and the World Series. We even got a few weekends off during the semester. These usually came after taking the SATs in nearby Oxnard. Since we lived so close, we usually brought a bunch of guys up to Lompoc. It was always a challenge for our parents to get us back to Malibu before the 6 p.m. deadline. Since many of the NWP guys were from out of state, we all chose to stay on campus for Thanksgiving. D helped cook that meal.*

*The afternoons were devoted to working out until dinner and the mandatory study hall. We spent quite a bit of time in the small shed behind the school that was the weight room. This was the same wooden shed that we helped empty when we got to NWP. There wasn't much room inside, so we would usually bring the weights outside. It was the only time I've been able to lift weights while looking at the ocean. Those were always great lifts. Sometimes firefighters from the nearby fire department would lift with us. We appreciated one gigantic fireman who was always providing pointers and critiquing our form. Derek, me and a few other guys had an ongoing bench competition. We all met our goal of benching 250 pounds by the end of that semester. NWP also had a field, basketball courts, and a pool. Your dad had his H2O polo ball and was always trying to teach people how to play his favorite game. He was one of the class PT instructors. He constantly motivated everyone to push themselves harder. He worked especially hard to help people who struggled with the physical stuff.*

*We spent many hours running on the PCH and the beach. We would use various rocky points on the coast as mile-markers. Just as I can't think of a nicer place to lift, I can't think of a nicer place to run. The onshore breeze made it easy to keep running. County Line is a pretty rural part of the coast. I'm sure the commuters wondered where all the shirtless teenagers running along the shoulders of the highway came from. A few miles north of NWP, near Pt. Magu State Beach, there is a huge sand dune. I remember running up and down that thing over and over with your Dad and some other guys. We would also run on the roads that led inland. One time were on one of these curvy two-lane roads when we saw a truck at the bottom of a cliff. We ran back and told the firemen, thinking someone might be trapped inside. Your dad was always thinking about others. We later found out that the truck was stolen and ditched there. Luckily, nobody was hurt.*

*As with most schooling, it is the times outside of class that are most clearly remembered. Derek's outrageous character highlights most of these memories for me. Living with a bunch of guys leads to a lot of joking around. Mr. Hoiby called this the famous game of braaboss. That was his fancy pronunciation of grabass. Derek was also a master of this game. Whether it was feeding the goats that roamed the campus food and toilet paper, or hosing people in the showers down with cold water, your Dad was there. He tried to lure those goats—Cornflake and Suffle'—into the dorms a few times, but the goats wouldn't fall for it. D punctuated the daily dorm wrestling battle royals with his crazy WWF moves. Never one to turn down a dare, he would also do crazy tricks like snorting tooth-floss up his nose until it came out of the back of his mouth. Perhaps his greatest performance came at the end of the semester in front of the whole school when he played the air-xylophone to the Cure's "Close to Me."*

*Below NWP, at the bottom of the hill, is a restaurant called Neptune's Net. The Net is a place that's only possible near L.A.*

*Part seafood diner, part greasy spoon—it's well known for the food, but more known for its clientele and laid back atmosphere. Nothing beats the Net's seafood. We hung out there quite a bit, usually during the weekends. We coexisted peacefully (most of the time) with the bikers, surfers, movie stars, and tourists.*

*Across the PCH from the Net is County Line Beach. We spent a lot of time there too. One time, one of our classmates supposedly irritated one of the locals. A rumor of a huge local versus preppie rumble quickly flooded the dorms. Within minutes a mob of preppies, most of who were still wearing polo shirts and Dockers came running down the hill to the Net. It probably looked ridiculous. Derek helped lead this charge, but unfortunately, or fortunately, there wasn't a gang of locals to rumble with.*

*A lot of movies, commercials, and ads are photographed or filmed around that area of the PCH. You can see the Net and County Line Beach in the quirky movie "Point Break." One day, some magazine was doing a photo shoot on the beach with model Kate Moss. A bunch of us were standing on the nearby bluff watching this spectacle. I was taking photos until Kate yelled at me to stop, and then flipped me off. We all got a big kick out of that.*

*After Northwestern, D and I went to Allan Hancock College in Santa Maria. We took the same classes and carpooled together. Eventually we found out that we would be going to Colorado that summer. We both probably took those dang SATs 9 or 10 times before finally getting the Academy minimums. That is just another example of how your Dad would never quit.*

*His sense of humor was the best. He didn't have to try very hard to get people to laugh. When he got his first tattoo, he told the artist that he wanted a shark with diving fins sticking out of its mouth. He wanted the shark to look like it had just eaten a body-boarder or diver. The artist didn't really get it. Listening to D trying to explain what he wanted was classic.*

*He was in our wedding. During the photos, the photographer had Derek stand on the floor with everyone else on a step behind him. He was still taller than everyone in the picture. I made sure the reception was well stocked with your dad's favorite . . . Coronas and lime. At the reception he had a cake fight with our oldest boy and instantly made a new friend. Things like that were normal for Derek and he made lots of friends, young and old alike. I laugh when I think of him and your Uncle Johnny singing songs at the reception. They were the life of the party. Your dad was always the life of the party.*

*He shook hands as every man should. In his handshake you could sense strength and sincerity. He would approach you with his big open hand, outstretched fingers, an amazing smile on his face and gleam in his eye. It was as if he was opening himself to you. When he gripped your hand, you knew you were shaking hands with a good man. At that moment you realized D would always be your bro. I'll miss shaking his hand and his bear hugs.*

*Years have passed since we drove down California Highway 1 to NWP. That day seems so far away now. Derek was an awesome man, a true hero. His sense of humor, attitude, loyalty, perseverance and dedication are examples for us all. He never gave up on his goals or took no for an answer. I never doubted that he would accomplish anything he set his mind to. I've always looked up to him and I always will. I will never forget. Love, B.J. July 2006*

BJ and Derek remained friends. After Derek's death, BJ spearheaded the project to place a memorial case for both Derek and Jeremy Fresques at the Academy. Both Todd Allison (who would later become my son-in-law and Logan's step-dad) and

I spoke the day they were unveiled in Colorado Springs. Both families were there and we are forever grateful to BJ, the AFA, the squadron and everyone who made this project possible. Many of the Combat Controllers flew out to be with us for the ceremony and to honor their brothers.

Another story from Northwestern Prep School came to me really by chance. Someone emailed me a little video from Memorial Day of 2011. It was a news clip from upper New York. On the clip, a Lt. Commander from the Navy was the speaker at a Memorial Day event. In the interview, he was speaking about Derek. He laughed during part of the interview, and held back his emotions too. I didn't know who he was, or how he knew Derek. The news station was able to put us in touch with each other. He wrote the following to share some humor about his time at NWP.

*Hello Logan,*

*My name is Joe Kato, and I knew your father for only a few months during the fall of 1995 while we were at Northwestern Prep School together in Malibu, CA. While we traded a few messages in the years after prep school, the last time I saw Derek was years ago before he joined the Air Force and I joined the Navy. The fact that I'm writing a letter and thinking about him so many years later is testament to how strong a personality he had and what a memorable guy he was. I hope this letter gives you a little insight into his personality as it was then.*

*While I've seen pictures of Derek all buffed up and decked out in equipment as a tough Air Force Captain, he'll forever in my mind be a tall, gangly, baby faced young man only a couple of months out of high school. All of us were young then, excited to be away from home, and eager to do anything and everything as quickly as we could. The school had a strict schedule and was regimented to improve our test scores. But, like any group of teenagers, we managed to find time to keep ourselves entertained with plenty of non-academic pursuits that make up 99% of my memories of that place. One particular memory should give you a good idea of your father's sense of humor.*

*Derek had the unique ability to eat anything ... ANYTHING! He was also broke, and needed spending money in a place where he had no ability to earn anything extra. That particular combination of talent and circumstance led to one incident that I still tell friends about. After a few days of hype, he held a fundraiser for himself by charging a few dollars for entrance to watch him eat a "substance". I believe the price of admission was $5.00 to watch, $10.00 to take pictures. While I will keep the identity of the substance to myself, I can tell you that I've never seen anyone else eat what he ate that day, and feel completely satisfied with my $5.00 purchase. Even though there was a little gaging, he made a show of it all and probably would have had a decent career option with the circus if he had decided to do that full time.*

*Although this may not be the most flattering story about your Dad, I hope that it conveys how much we all enjoyed his company. He was full of life and exciting to be around because he was never boring.*

*Very Respectfully, Joseph J. Kato May 2010 Lt. Commander, U.S. Navy*

This is a story from the Air Force Academy Prep school about Derek's humor. I met Reina by chance at your Mom and your Dad Todd's wedding, later in 2009. She attended the Air Force Academy Prep School also. Derek called me once from the prep school, as he often did, and expressed concern that they might dismiss him for some reason or another. He told me on that call that he had whistled at a female cadet. I always wondered who she was. She introduced herself to me at the wedding and said she had a little story for me. I was excited and said, "Oh no, are you the cadet he whistled at?"

*Dear Logan,*

*I wanted to share with you a story of your Dad that I think you would like. It brings a smile to my face when I think about it. I went to the Air Force Academy with your Dad and Todd. Todd and I were B-Squad and your Dad was in A. One afternoon at the Prep School we had a fire alarm. I had just got out of the shower and was still in my bathrobe when my roommate said we needed to get outside as fast as possible. I wasn't excited about this idea because I knew I was going to be the only person in a bathrobe as I headed outside with my roommate. I knew I was going to get a few laughs as soon as I left the building. Without disappointment, there were a bunch of guys that whistled as I made my way to the back of the formation. I wasn't really surprised. They released us and we all went back to our rooms to start on some homework. Later one of the MTL's showed up at my room with a couple of guys. One of them was Pierre and the other was your Dad. Apparently, after we all left formation the MTL asked those that whistled to come forward and apologize. I know there were a lot of people that whistled, but your Dad and Pierre were the only ones with courage to come forward. The whistling didn't really bother me, but it impressed me that Derek and Pierre came to me and said sorry. It is probably just another example of what a great guy your Dad is and how he always tried to do the right thing, even if it wasn't easy. Lots of Love, Reina (April 2009)*

Derek was human and tried to make the best of prep school with a little humor here and there. He never took his eyes off of the goal however. The AFA prep school does not insure that you will get an appointment to the academy. This letter comes from

Brendan, who attended the prep school and the academy with Derek.

> *Derek was one of the most motivated people I've ever met. He was dedicated, driven and determined in everything he did: from playing basketball to preparing for inspections to encouraging his classmates through difficult times. Once in a while, there'll be a person whom everyone he or she comes in contact with admires. Derek was that person. Without saying a word, he commanded respect from his peers, subordinates, and superiors in the chain of command. His stature placed him literally above average, but it was his personality we all looked up to.*
>
> *Derek was the type of person we read about; learning how to model his style of leadership, fellowship, and his perseverance at them both. He was the type you'd gladly follow into combat; for whom you'd do anything.*
>
> *Strong as he was, he was kind, unselfish, gentle, and noble. Derek was a living collage of paradoxes: the sensitive jock, the gentle giant, the servant leader. I miss him . . . we all do.*
>
> *Derek was a prime example of leading by example. The example he always set was excellence. You knew he was going above and beyond and you wanted to do the same. He was one of those people you didn't want to let down. Not that he would belittle you if you did, but you always knew he was giving his best and you felt guilty, almost selfish, around him if you weren't. He wasn't perfect, I mean, who is? But he was on that path, realizing it was a "journey and not a destination" as Arthur Ashe referred to the path of success. I guess that's why he was always in motion, always moving toward one goal or another. To know him implied he'd left his imprint of excellence in your heart and mind. Brendan June 2006*

# Four

Department of The Air Force
Headquarters United States Air Force Academy
USAF Academy Colorado

Memorandum For Whom It May Concern
From: CIC Derek M. Argel, (CS02, X453)
Subject: Letter of Request for the Special Tactics Career Field

The reason I would like to be in Special Tactics is because I want a career Combat Control. I have prepared my whole life for the opportunity to get a chance to try out for this elite unit. I came to the Air Force Academy for an education and to play water polo, but I want a life in the CCT career field. I attended mini-BUD/s this summer in hopes of proving that I have what it takes both mentally and physically to succeed in this type of career. I was one out of three chosen in my class of 36 to return to BUD/S.

I feel I am physically qualified for the job. I have been playing water polo for 10 years. I am an avid runner and I have maxed the Academy's physical fitness test. I am also a patriot and my heart lies in defending our country. I serve in the military because I feel I owe my country a service. I came to the Air Force Academy because I want to serve my country in an Air Force uniform. I'm looking for a challenge that is both physical and mental. I know that the Special Tactics will be able to provide me with both.

I am committed to becoming a Special Tactics Officer. I have been preparing myself for an opportunity to get to try out. When I attended mini-BUD/S this summer, I became more aware of what it was going to take to get through the toughest military training in the world. I recently talked with the proctor of the mini-BUD/S program and he asked if I would be returning. I also received an email from LCDR ____ who is in charge of training at the BUD/S compound. He asked me if I would be returning and said he would do whatever it takes to help me return to BUD/S. When SEAL instructors take a personal interest in my career choice, it makes me just that much more focused. I told them I would be looking into Special Tactics first because they have what I need to test my abilities beyond what I have seen before. I hope that I am given this opportunity.

I am uniquely qualified for this position. I should be given the opportunity to try out for the Special Tactics career field. I have both the mental fortitude and the physical stamina to be the best Combat Control officer out there.

DEREK M. ARGEL, CIC, USAFA
ELEMENT LEADER, CADET SQUADRON TWO

The letter above was written from the Air Force Academy by Derek asking for the chance to try out for Special Tactics in the Air Force. The next letter talks about what happened at mini-BUD/S. It is a story about loyalty and of course, humor.

*Dear Logan,*

*I met your father, Derek, on the 26th of June 1997 in Basic Cadet Training at the Air Force Academy. I knew him well for the next four years of our lives. I wanted to write this letter to share some of the good times we had together and show you what a profound influence Derek had on my life.*

*Throughout Basic Training Derek stood out as the natural leader of our group of 30 basic cadets. He was always the big dude out in front with the low voice who would never quit. Whatever physical event we did, whether it was running through the obstacle course, daily running, push-ups, sit-ups, playing sports, etc., Derek was always the best. Moreover, he wasn't the guy who would finish first and look down on everybody as inferior. Rather, he was humble and would use his physical prowess to motivate everybody else to work just as hard as him and perform to the best of their abilities. He took a lot of flack from the cadre in charge. They would tease him for being so big, or thinking he was so tough or having to go through two prep schools to get here, etc. The reason why he often got singled out is because he had thick skin and could take it very well. Derek would then make fun of the cadre right back to their faces. They respected him for all of these reasons. Standing out in front and being a leader like Derek always was, often means that you are the one who everybody focuses on—it just comes with the job, which is why being a great leader is such a difficult task. At the end of Basic Training, he was awarded a Commandant's Award, which was a silver wreath given to the top 5 of our group of 30.*

*Initially I had aspirations of cross-commissioning to the Army, but training with Derek and another cadre during Basic Training, (now a Navy SEAL), convinced me that I had the ability to be better than an Army grunt, rather I could be a Special Operator. One problem, however, was that I was not a swimmer, and water confidence and swimming ability were necessary skills to enter the Special Operations community. In fact, I remember as a young freshman going to the pool and being unable to swim more than 25m without hanging on the wall and gasping for breath. Holding my breath underwater seemed impossible to do for more than 5 seconds. In spite of working out countless hours with the water polo team, attending a full schedule of classes, taking care of his military duties, and studying, Derek always made time to teach me about swimming and water confidence whenever I asked. That precious time he spent helping me in the water paid huge dividends for my personal training. Within 2 years, I was swimming competitively in triathlons, and felt very confident underwater.*

*During the off-season our first two years at the Academy, Derek and I would work out doing calisthenics, running, swimming, and other training together. I always looked forward to those workouts, because I was constantly motivated by him, and we would always push each other to be better.*

*During our junior year at the Academy, the two of us went through a selection process to determine who would attend the mini-BUD/S (Basic Underwater Demolition/SEAL) training at Coronado NAS, CA. There were initially 23 of our classmates who showed interest, but only 5 of us were selected to attend the course. Derek and I were the only two Air Force Academy representatives in the first of the two mini-BUD/S classes that year.*

*Navy SEAL training was known as "the toughest military training in the world." The washout rate of students was from 80-95%. A typical BUD/S class would start out with 150 extremely motivated men and would graduate 10-20. Mini-BUD/S was an officer selection course where the enlisted SEAL instructors placed the participants (all cadets/*

*midshipmen who were one year out from graduating and becoming officers) through similar training to the actual BUD/S course. The enlisted instructors would then hand-pick the officers from mini-BUD/S to enter BUD/S one year later and eventually lead them into combat.*

*Derek picked me up at San Diego airport the night before we were supposed to report to mini-BUD/S. My bags were lost on the flight over, and Derek forgot his blue's flight cap. Derek loaned me BDU's which were too large for me, and although it clearly did not fit me, I decided it would be better than wearing no uniform. We shopped around for a blue flight cap for Derek, but we couldn't find one on that naval base. Were we intimidated showing up in an incorrect uniform on the first day of the toughest military training in the world? Derek surely wasn't and thus I wasn't. We wandered around until we found our instructors and reported in. They gave us a hard time as we stood there at attention in our uniforms. Derek asked if they were going to give us Navy uniforms to wear throughout the program, and the instructor replied, "yes." Derek then asked "Are you going to have something in my size," as he broke down from the position of attention and started flexing and of course, smiling and laughing. The look on the Instructor's face was absolutely priceless. He just stood there for a second with his mouth open unable to believe that a brand new guy just made this joke. This was followed shortly by the Instructor bursting out laughing and calling all of the other SEAL instructors around to introduce them to us and inform them of Derek's joke. We, of course, were doing lots of pushups after that, but what a way to make a first impression.*

*Derek and I were roommates and did most everything together for the next 4 weeks. We hung out in San Diego in our free time, we partied together, we ate every meal together, and we spent a lot of time in the room just talking. I got to know him very well during those 4 weeks. I was so impressed with how highly he regarded his family and how close he was with them. We lived in the same barracks as all the other Navy cadets going through the program with us, as well as the seamen going through the actual BUD/S program. The Navy participants all bragged about how difficult it was for them to make it to mini-BUD/S and initially treated us like we had no right to be here. The Naval Academy cadets would claim that only 10,000 men would apply for the Naval Academy each year, mostly to become SEALS. Only 1,000 of those highly qualified people would be accepted to enter the Academy. Then, they said that about 500 cadets in the beginning of their junior year would try for the 28 total slots for the two sessions of mini-BUD/S—all claiming they had to be in the top .28% to get here. The Navy ROTC students claimed there were over 1,000 people competing in the beginning of the year for their 28 slots. Regardless, it only took a short amount of time before Derek convinced them that although he didn't have to compete against hundreds of people to get here, he was still much better and more deserving than they were.*

*The first formal event of the training was taking a PT test. Derek and I both maxed out the pull-ups, pushups, and sit ups together. In the pool, however Derek finished the swim faster than anybody there—including two All American swimmers from the Naval Academy. He did so well the instructors started taking bets on how poorly he would perform in the next event, the run. They all assumed that a big, built guy would not be able to run as fast as the skinny guy—which is usually a safe bet. Besides, they said, he must have put all of his energy into the swim? Wrong again, Derek finished the run first place again, in front of another All American track athlete from Navy ROTC.*

*Throughout the program, the instructors would often single Derek and I out, as "the Air Force guys," for extra harassment. No matter what they did, Derek would reply that the Air Force*

Academy produces the "toughest men alive." The two of us sure got "wet and sandy" a lot and did a lot of extra calisthenics for these comments, but Derek really was the toughest—he knew it, he backed it up, it could never be beaten out of him. Most importantly, he would always be grinning as he made his toughest man alive comments—he always kept his sense of humor throughout, no matter how stressful the situation.

Derek has always been a loyal friend and a specific event in our water training highlights for me his extreme loyalty. Throughout the water confidence portions of the training, due in large part to Derek's help three years earlier, we both excelled. Among many of the water confidence events, we were tied up (our hands and feet) and thrown in 12 feet of water and told to survive, we treaded water with weights, and we tied knots at 15' under water—all the while the instructors harassed us. I was feeling pretty confident at 15' below the water, and after I successfully tied and untied my knot, rather than letting me go back up for air my instructor gave me the finger telling me that he was going to keep me down there till I passed out. I wasn't intimidated, so I flicked him off. That instructor who I flicked off laughed about it and gave me a "bring it on" underwater—later when I talked to him he thought it was a pretty gutsy move of mine. However, another instructor who was unaware of the situation thought that I was showing disrespect towards them by flicking them off. As I got out of the water, this other instructor grabbed me and started to make my life extremely miserable. In fact, this instructor was so irate about the "disrespect" I had shown that he wanted to kick me out of the course. The other Navy midshipmen/cadets around would do nothing about the unfair situation I was in, and this instructor was not listening to my side of the story. (Meanwhile, the instructor I flicked off was still working with other students underwater oblivious to my situation). Honestly, that was the most scared I was throughout the entire program. Just because

*I am confident enough to do something like that underwater, I was getting kicked out of this program I had worked so hard for the last 3 years of my life? Derek apparently saw me from the other side of the pool and immediately came running across to help me out. He didn't even know my situation, but he was there right next to me to back me up. As we were both doing pushups and crawling around the pool and getting yelled at, I told Derek my situation. He literally stepped up and confronted this other instructor, telling him that the situation was bullshit and I meant no disrespect. I couldn't seem to get this message through when I told the instructor this, but when Derek stepped up the instructor left me alone. In my darkest hour at this program, Derek came to my side immediately, not knowing my situation initially and having nothing to gain for himself. He kept me out of a lot of trouble and potentially kept me in the mini-BUD/S program, all because he is such a loyal friend.*

*Although Derek's physical ability was the best of all participants in this program, testing our pure physical ability wasn't the reason we were out here. A Navy SEAL friend of mine before the program told me that he had seen plenty of All American athletes who could run, swim, and do more pushups than anyone yet were mentally unable to make it through even a day of BUD/S training. He explained that the best SEAL is not necessarily the guy who can physically do the most work, but who is the mentally toughest. He said that when they are out in the field for weeks at a time in some of the worst, most stressful conditions, it is your mental toughness that gets the job done. For the entire four week program, day in and day out, Derek proved he was not just the physically toughest, but the mentally toughest also as well as the best leader of our class.*

*Derek had many opportunities to prove his mental toughness such as "hell day" where we were awake doing physically exhausting exercises for 36 straight hours with no sleep. We also constantly carried around heavy zodiac boats on our heads until our necks felt like they would snap and the skin would wear off the top of our heads with the constant rubbing (and Derek was the tallest in his boat crew, causing that much more pain). Maybe it was the fact that the sand which coated our clothes inside and out would chafe all the skin on our body causing painful blisters and rashes on our skin and extreme pain for every tiny movement. Perhaps it was the freezing cold ocean we would simply stand in until we were hypothermic, shaking uncontrollably, and barely able to see or think strait. During conditions like these, I personally witnessed countless "tough guys" break down mentally, usually starting to cry or getting extremely irritable and turning on their friends. These guys' toughness was obviously just a show. These are the times when you can see deep into another person, who they really are and what they are made of. Regardless of what sort of training they put us through Derek could never be mentally broken down, ever. This was the case because his character, his soul, his desire to be the best and serve his country was the essence of Derek, not just an act. That is why even in the worst of conditions everybody would look to Derek as a leader. His level head, constant motivation, combined with his sense of humor even in the worst of times made everybody in our group desire to follow whatever he said. This is what everybody including the SEAL instructors and I saw that summer in mini-BUD/S. This is why although both of us were invited back, the SEALS kept calling and emailing Derek personally all year long begging him to come back and be one of them. Sadly, it was the politicians of much higher rank in the Navy, rather than the enlisted SEALS, who would decide if Air Force cadets could become SEALS this year.*

*Following our experiences in Coronado, the five of us who had previously gone to mini-BUD/S were in charge of running the screening process for the cadets in the year group below us to attend another summer of mini-BUD/S. Derek and I were the only two who really stepped up and set up a good training and selection program for those below us. We both put countless hours in to ensure that the class below us showed up to mini BUD/S as well prepared as us and as all the classes from the Academy had been for years before. During the final screening session, I offered the others some advice about how to excel at the program, good luck, etc. After me, Derek stood up and made the most inspirational speech I have ever heard. He talked about the fact that he is here for love of his country and its protection and defense—the purest of motives. He mentioned that he is not the most military "looking" member because he doesn't think having an ironed shirt and shined shoes leads to the defense of the nation or including the Americans he loves, such as his mother at home. Oftentimes, he said, those people are the biggest cowards as they hide behind a nice uniform yet are not capable of any real action which would lead to the defense of the nation. Even worse, these people sometimes take away our ability to defend with their non-common sense thinking, and he would never be one of them. Derek said, however, that when things really do matter and his actions will affect the safety of America, he will be the first one there, he will stand up and be counted, and he will lay down his life if needed. You could tell from the look in his eye and his tone of voice that he meant every word of it. There was a silence in the pool for the next 4-5 minutes as we were all speechless following his words. I can't put into words what that speech meant to me, and when I talked to the others later they all felt the exact same. I can merely say that I was so inspired that I wrote down a few notes to remember it forever.*

*Following graduation from the Air Force Academy, I regretfully lost touch with Derek. Other than a few emails here and there, our schedule never enabled us to hold up the friendship too well—that is my biggest regret. Derek, of course, continued down the Special Operations road in the Combat Control career field, and went on to much bigger and better things than I have described here. I, on the other hand, chose to fly. I am now an F-16 pilot, and write this while I am serving in Iraq. Every day, I wake up and am proud to use my F-16 to serve and help out the Special Operators like Derek on the ground.*

*Hopefully these few simple and objective stories show why when I think of Derek what comes to mind is his extraordinary common sense (sounds funny, but it is so important and so rare), and his sense of humor. His leadership, his loyalty, his friendship, and his deep love of country are the reason why in my senior photo of the AFA yearbook I mentioned Derek by name. I will continue to be inspired for the rest of my life by my friendship with Derek, and I will attempt to live these same values which he so well exemplified.*

*By the time you read this Logan, I don't know what history will have to say about the War on Terrorism, and I don't care to predict. Understand what I am telling you is from a guy who is here in Iraq, with a need-to-know, top-secret security clearance—not some college professor or news reporter who can make up whatever facts they want because they are so far removed from the actual situation in Iraq. What you need to know is that first, there are tons of terrorists out there who are trying to kill us as Americans. Secondly, America is winning the war in Iraq and preventing these terrorists from attacking America—note there have been no attacks on US soil since September 11$^{th}$, 2001. Finally, and most importantly, as an F-16 pilot I see and support many of the operations which your Dad ran in Iraq every day and every night. The operations of Special Operators like your Dad are the reason why America is safe. Your dad successfully fought for and achieved freedom for Americans. He is truly a hero and America should be grateful for the work he did. Capt. Michael June 2006*

This is one of the most profound and insightful letters into your Dad's character I have read. The issue of the "uniform" would come up many times during Derek's time at the Academy and in other events. I should pause to explain that when Derek gave his talk at the pool, he had just been to his brother's graduation ceremony from basic at Lackland AFB, in San Antonio, TX. Johnny had returned from Chaminade University in Honolulu and decided to join the Air Force. Derek rushed out with special permission to support him. That was his only focus that day. Derek wore his AFA uniform to the ceremony, after which we went to a local mall for lunch. We were met by a rather chubby officer there who took the time to come to our table and verbally reprimand Derek for the wrinkled state of his uniform. Derek took it in stride, apologized and didn't make excuses. Shortly after the ceremony Derek wrote to his brother from the Academy.

**Dear Johnny,**

**Excuse the typing, but I type faster than I can write so bear with. I think about a subject very often. Sometimes it pains me and sometimes I think to myself should I bother, but I've come to the conclusion that it does bother me. You probably don't realize this too much John, but you are inspiration for everything I do. Growing up watching you participate in athletics, I idolized you. "Johnny Argel can do anything." It almost sickened me to think about it, no matter what I did I would never amount to the athlete that you were and are. I loved to watch you play water polo and I loved to watch you swim, I even loved to watch you play basketball, you weren't that good, but there was something about the way you did different sports that just made me want to be like you. I knew that I would never play water polo like John Argel, but if I practiced hard enough I would come close. That's bullshit and I'll tell you why, the one**

thing I learned from you growing up Johnny was that I should never strive to be like anyone else, I should be the guy other people strive to be. I began to develop my own style of play, I began to develop my own personality but I'll never forget who my mentor was and still is.

You have made a lot of mistakes in your life, but nothing I would never be willing to forgive you about and that is for one reason, because of guidance you have given me throughout my years. You really have no idea how I feel about you John. I don't have to go out on the weekends and party, or find big social settings to make me happy. I can sit alone with my thoughts and think about the things that we've done together. I often ask myself why I'm built the way I am. There is one person at the top of the pyramid that I can think of and that's you. My wisdom has come from you. Do you remember the relationship we had growing up, I can recall many times when we wouldn't talk or hang out. It wasn't till about my junior year that I finally became part of the crew, which was about the time we began to bond.

You may be asking yourself why I'm writing this letter. It's for a very good reason. It was John Argel that started me playing water polo. It was John Argel that introduced me to the idea of Navy SEALS and that got me started on a journey that has put me closer than anyone other than myself could have. It is John Argel that has helped me get through some of the toughest years of my life. It is John Argel whom I'm still striving to be. John, you will never comprehend the feeling that consumed me when I first saw you in your blues. You will never understand what it felt like to sit in those stands and watch as you marched proudly by. You will never know the feeling of guilt that I have not been able to tell the man that started me on

> **my quest that he should be here and I should be there. You deserve better, correct that, you are better than what you're doing. I hope you find what you are looking for soon. I love you and will respect you whatever you decide. John, I will always be here for you as you have been there for me. You give me inspiration and hope and I'm proud to be your brother. Love, D**

John and Derek were very close brothers. Derek was never too proud to tell the people he loved how he felt. Like all brothers they had their moments, but most of the time they were laughing together or trading funny jibes. After basic Johnny headed for the base in Washington to begin his training. During his training, he received the following email from Derek.

> **"Hey Johnny,**
>
> **How are things right about now? Nothing too hard yet is there? We are all getting ready for recognition here. Next week the Frosh are going to be accepted as upperclassmen. How is the training going? I'm pretty stoked on going to mini-BUDs this summer, only I'm not sure if I'm keeping myself in the best shape. Well, I hope you are kicking some arse up there. I know if you really do well, you can get an honors graduate spot. Will there be anything like that in your future? You have to keep up tradition. It also must be hard lugging that belly around. Have you gotten rid of that yet? I'm hoping you are a lean mean machine. How is the food there anyway? I'd like to know how things are going with you. I hope you don't mind the typing either, I type faster than I write and I'm about to go to lunch so I'm trying to hurry. Mid-semester grades come out this week and for the first time in a long time, I might be above a 3.0. I would definitely be stoked. Water polo practice started**

**yesterday. Too much swimming, it sucks. Well bro, I'm gonna send you a few pics and a few jokes to keep you amused.**

**Take care bro, you make me proud. Love, D"**

The boys stayed in touch as often as possible with their schedules in both training and at the Air Force Academy. As always, the three of us were always together for the holidays.

*Ma'am,*

*I knew Derek for three years while I was at the Academy. He was 1 year behind me at school. I am currently a Combat Rescue Officer stationed at Kadena AB, Okinawa. I drank a few beers with Jeremy Fresques a few days prior to the incident while I was deployed in Africa. His Combat Control Team came down to do some work and I met up with them in Djibouti.*

*I originally had planned on leaving the AF when graduating the Academy and going to the Navy to become a SEAL. The selection process is quite strenuous. The pain and instruction inflicted on us gets passed down to the next class land so on. I had the luxury and the honor to put both Derek and Jeremy through some tough Friday night sessions. 20 '01ers showed up for the first session, and out of them 4 knew they would be selected to go to "Mini-BUD/S." Basically the course at Coronado would end up being Officer Candidate selection for SEALS.*

*I knew from day one that Derek had what it takes to become a SEAL. I was prior-enlisted in USAF Para-rescue (still a student when selected for USAFA) so I have been through some pretty tough schools. No matter what stresses and exercises we had put the guys through, Derek always had that smile on his face; the one little smirk that basically told us he wanted more!!! I thought I was in phenomenal shape back then and here was a guy who could match me in every exercise, and then some!!! I wouldn't dare step into the pool with him for any water event! I'm not sure if it was from surfing at Northwestern or playing Division One water polo, but you could tell he wasn't phased by anything in the pool.*

*The one memory that quickly entered my mind when I had heard the news on 1 June, 2005, was Derek standing tall at the pool. (USN LT S, SEAL Tm 10) were "smoking" the class. Physically breaking them on the side of the pool with thousands of push-ups and flutter-kicks. I remember walking back and forth screaming at these guys when Derek smiled at me. They were in the middle of their flutter-kicks when this happened. We were friends and I told him that during this selection, stuff like this wouldn't fly. He then proceeded to remove his hand from his underside and "val salva." This is where you clear your ears by pinching your nose (in this case he was wearing a scuba mask filled with water) and exert pressure by blowing air out of your nose. I saw him do this right in front of me, smiling . . . when all of the sudden, bubbles were pouring out of his eye. I will never forget his face because there were a lot of other guys there, all in pain, struggling to keep up with the cadence of the exercise; and here was Derek, smiling, not phased by the number of flutter kicks, and blowing "bubbles" out of his eye socket!!! After that night, Drew, Gage (Helo Pilot), Leo (F-15s), and myself were laughing so hard about that incident. Derek always had some trick or joke to tell which set the mood. That night was early on in the selection process, and all of us knew after that session that we were definitely sending him to Coronado.*

*I try so terribly hard to remember the good times Derek and I had at the Academy, and I am ashamed that this is the only memory that comes to mind. He reminded me of myself but a year behind. I remember "smoking" the upper-classmen in PT during Basic Training as a Cadet, and I heard great stories of him doing the same. He had the perfect attitude and outlook. I could tell that somewhere he would find his place in the military. I knew he had gotten married when I spoke with Mark back at Yuma, AZ when Mark and I were going through Free-fall together. I didn't know he had a little boy. Please pass on to Logan a big hug from me.*

*Derek left this earth much too young, and will never be forgotten. He is truly one of the greatest guys I have ever met, and I only wish I could have gotten to know him more. With Utmost Sincerity, Mark July 2007*

The daily rigors at the Academy, combined with sports is very taxing. Your dad worked hard to make sure he never lost focus. He was the first to admit when he made a mistake and took great pains to correct them. Another great letter out of the Academy adds a little humor to another uniform situation.

*Dear Ms. Bastian,*

*First let me apologize in how long it has taken me to complete this letter. Obviously, I saw your request for stories about Derek on the memorial webpage some time ago. Unfortunately, I must fall back on the lame excuse that the TDY rate is still high and I have spent the majority of the last year overseas. May 30 was a workday for us this year. I had just returned from an overseas trip. I was mindful of the anniversary, amazed that a year had passed, and not in much mood to do office work. There are a number of 2001 graduates in my squadron, and there was a noticeable pall at work that day. I greeted one as we sat down to work. "How's it going?" He stared at me and cocked his head. "I can't believe it's been a year." I nodded. One of or office-mates, not a graduate, wanted to know what it had been a year since, and we told him that two of our friends had been killed in Iraq.*

Obviously this is not common in the Air Force, even among us pilots, and he shrank back, apologetic about something he had little way of knowing.

Word spread quickly on the day after last year. I got an e-mail first thing in the morning, West Coast time, from Paul, whom I'd gone to high school with in southern California, and who had played water polo at the Academy with Derek, graduating in 1999. I stared at it, thinking that obviously there was some huge mistake. They must have had the wrong name. But after a minute or two of staring at the computer, a quick Google search revealed that Col Heidmous' forwarded message was, in fact, not a fantastic error. I reached for the phone.

My call was to Lauren, my best friend from USAFA, who had been in CS-36 with Derek during basic training and our freshman and sophomore year. I had been in CS-37 just down the hall.

"Lauren, I'm sending you an e-mail I just got. Derek's gone." I explained what I had read about the plane crash.

"What?" she said. "No, you must be wrong. It must be some kind of mistake. Mr. Indestructible can't die."

In setting some background, so far this letter has been about me and the 2001 classmates I was stationed at McChord AFB, WA, with. For that I apologize, but Lauren's comment about Mr. Indestructible is the only way to start some of the stories I remember about Derek.

We really did call him Mr. Indestructible. As I said, I spent the first two years at the Academy living just down the way from Derek, Lauren and the other Pink Panthers of CS-36. In basic training, the quarters had been even tighter as we all lived in tents together out in Jack's Valley. Derek's stature marked him from the beginning, but for most of us, it was only a split second after we noticed how tall he was that we noticed the little smile that always played across his face. A lot of the time, it was half-smile, half-smirk, kind of like, "I've got a joke!" You'd be surprised how much of a comfort the smirk-smile grew to be to us as exhausted basics. The upperclassmen had gravitated toward Derek initially, but it also didn't seem to take them long to figure out that, unlike most of the rest of us, he just didn't seem to have a point of physical exhaustion, at least not one they could reach. Not for lack of trying, though. Throughout it all, the smirk-smile was always present. No matter what they did to us, no matter how dirty and tired we all were, Derek wore that little smile. Maybe because we knew he was a couple years older and probably knew more about the game, it got to be a comfort. I thought that if he could take all of this abuse and cruise through it with a smile on his face, then I could suck it up a little more.

After basic training, things settled into their normal routine. Over the next four years, I saw Derek in passing just about every day. Usually it was down at the gym while we were both lifting, or while I and the rest of the women's cross-country ski team were running laps around the gym and looking forward to the west side, where we would run past the window that overlooked the pool where the water polo boys practiced, or on the walk back up to Mitchell Hall after practice to get dinner. We would say hello and continue on our way. We didn't really run in the same social circles, so for the most part that was the extent of my interaction with him.

First year, we both took the same course on joint warfare. It was a small class, one that I had picked because I had met and liked the instructor and figured that he would make it interesting. I assumed that Derek had elected it since at that point, we all knew he was trying to go combat control. I was glad to see him. In four years, I don't think we'd had any previous classes together, but I remember thinking that he would definitely make it more fun.

On the first day of class, the instructor closed the door precisely at start time and looked around the room. His name was Major Jeff, and he was a pretty hard-core Army air assault pilot. As it turned out, he also took a great personal interest in every one of his students, more so than any other instructor I ever had there. He already seemed to know a lot about us. The first day was mostly administrative, having us fill out some cards with personal info, passing out the course lists, etc. Toward the end of the class, he looked up at the clock.

"I need a class timekeeper," he announced. "I need someone who'll keep good track throughout the semester and let me know exactly when it's time to start and end the class. I would also like a 5-minute warning from the end of each period so I can wrap things up and make sure I let you guys go on time." His eyes swept the room and settled on Derek. "Cadet Argel." Derek was seated immediately behind me, and I turned around to look at him. He smiled.

"Sir, I don't have a watch," he explained politely. I didn't know whether he meant he didn't have one that day, or didn't have one at all. The Major's eyes narrowed and he pointed a finger at Derek. "Officers wear watches," he said crisply. We were less than six months away from graduating and being commissioned. It was becoming more and more real to us, not just an abstract responsibility we would assume at some distant, fuzzy point in the future. It was right around the corner, and we were all intimidated by it, and determined to do what we could to do a good job and do right by the enlisted who would be under our command. But at the same time, I knew of Derek's reputation as a jokester and that like most of us, he had little patience for silly little rules that didn't seem to have mission impact. I turned *around again, expecting to see Derek wearing the smirk-smile. The smile was still there, but it was blank, like he was trying to hide what he was thinking. He wasn't completely successful though. Behind the smile he looked a little bit crestfallen at this perceived rebuke, at having disappointed the Major. Two days later the class met again and he sported a large digital watch, and he functioned as the timekeeper for the rest of the semester.*

*It was an enjoyable class. We learned a lot about the different services and ran through a large theoretical joint exercise. Every now and then, usually on a Friday or on some day immediately preceding a long weekend or break when he knew we probably wouldn't pay much attention anyway, The Major would come in and say, "I don't feel like teaching the course material today, and I'm pretty sure you don't feel like listening. You're all big boys and girls and you can do the reading on your own. Today is war story day." Each time he'd bring in another officer on the faculty who had combat experience, or who had leadership wisdom to impart, or he would tell his own stories. We listened, fascinated. A couple of times we were so into it that Derek forgot the 5 minute warning and we would go over, not that it bothered any of us. The morning after we had been informed through official channels what our AFSC's would be, the Major congratulated each of us without asking what we had gotten. He had gone and found out. The last day of class, the Major was in his full Army dress uniform and gave a special presentation. He had gone through the yearbook files and found all of our pictures from freshman year, and contrasted them with a slide following that had our graduation pictures, and then one that had what we were going to do in the Air Force (or in the Marines, for the guy who was cross-commissioning). Since the smile was ever present on Derek's face, I remember being kind of surprised that he hadn't smiled in his graduation photo and looked pretty severe. The Major had hand-made plaques for all of us, covered in camouflage material, with the name-tape of the service we were being commissioned into, Second Lieutenant's rank, and a dog-tag onto which he'd engraved his best wishes. We were all humbled to be honored this way by someone whom we had all come to admire very much, and it had the air of ceremony. I don't know what everyone else did with theirs. I have held onto mine throughout several moves, and it's the only Air Force award I keep displayed in my office, since it came from someone I respect and who I knew cared about me and my classmates. When Derek's turn came, he accepted the plaque and looked at the floor when the Major announced that he would be a combat control officer. "Well," he said, "I haven't done it yet."*

*He did it though, and from what I heard later he did a great job at it, keeping up that Mr. Indestructible reputation.*

*I ran into him some time during Graduation Week. I think it was right before or right after one of the parades, or maybe even right after the graduation ceremony during the Thunderbird show, since we were all milling around in our parade dress and feeling ecstatic. We congratulated each other and hugged, and I wished him good luck in the indoc course, since I figured he needed good wishes for that more than I needed them for pilot training. That was the last time I ever saw him in person, although I later saw some pictures in a magazine from CCT training.*

*Derek's memory will stay with the many of us whom he impressed and inspired. God Bless, Stephanie, June 2008*

I remember Derek's call to me the day that he was chosen as the timekeeper. He would need a little money to pay back the person who gave him a loan for the watch. From that time on, he always wore at least one watch. When he was in the field he usually wore two. I had visited this class that Stephanie wrote about. During parent's weekend each year, the parent's had the opportunity to go to class with their cadet. The cadets would introduce their parents to the class and to the instructor. As was so typical of Derek's humor, he introduced me as his sister and not his mother, which drew a laugh from the other cadets. He was near graduation. He had come from academic probation in his freshman year to the Dean's list. He had helped others get to that point, and talked countless cadets into braving it out when they thought about leaving. He had shared his personal story with only a few.

# Five

When Derek was about six he used to point at dogs and ask if they would bite. I developed a standard answer. "All dogs bite and all guns are loaded", I would tell him. The answer seemed reasonable and satisfied him at the time. I would often go skeet shooting at the range near La Purisima Mission with my father. Johnny and Derek became interested in learning to shoot also. The range provided a basic hunter safety course for kids. They took the course and I purchased 22 chipmunk rifles for them. It was a small, light single shot rifle. It was during one of their target sessions that I first noticed a little twitch in Derek's right hand. It was very slight, but noticeable. He learned to control it, but it was still there. We had the doctor check it out. The doctor detected a small valve problem in his heart, but said that he would outgrow it and it was nothing to worry about. It would come back to haunt him years later, but he would overcome it just as he did with other obstacles in his path.

In the spring of the Junior year, the cadets are given another full and complete physical as they begin to make their career choices and the lists are formed for flight school, etc. Not long after the physical, I received a call. The voice on the other end could barely speak to utter the words, "Ma . . . . they want to drop me." I knew right away that the heart problem had surfaced again. The valve problem had become a little more intense. "Are you going to fight this son?" I asked, knowing the answer would be yes. He would be sent to San Antonio in the next couple of days. He would spend about one week out there for specific tests on his heart and to wear a monitor around for about four days. I could tell by the tone in his voice that it would be the longest week of his life. Two prep schools to get there, working his grades up the ladder, the sports schedule and the intense hours of trying to help others achieve their own goals, but mostly his dreams.

Each day he was in San Antonio we talked a couple of times daily. He was wearing the monitor around to see the tourist sites and trying to make those excruciatingly long days a little shorter. The night before the monitor came off, I remember that he called to say goodnight and "Wish me luck!" I said, "Son, luck has nothing to do with it. If anyone can talk their way into staying in and making a case for yourself, it is you!"

It was a long night of no sleep and lots of prayer. I waited by the phone the next day and told anyone that called that I had to leave the line open. Finally, the phone rang. He could tell how anxious I was to hear the news either way. "Well" he began. I waited for the long pause to end and felt the news he was going to give me was not good. "What did they say", I pressed. His voice picked up to a high level of enthusiasm. "They said I am going to break their treadmill!" "Ma, they passed me and I'm heading back to the academy today!" That night, I had a couple of friends over to celebrate and I thanked God for getting us over this hurdle. Only a few at the Academy would know the anguish of the last week for Derek and they were praying for him too.

Back at the Academy, he went back to his normal routine which was anything but normal as all of those know that have graduated from any academy. The schedule was back breaking. You finish in four years or you don't finish. Part of the routine as an upper classman was serving as cadre to the younger cadets. When Derek was a freshman he was constantly harassed by one particular cadre. As Derek described it, he was only about waist high to Derek. One evening after a long day of classes and water polo practice, he came back down the hall to see all of his belongings tossed out into the hall by this gentleman. The cadre proceeded to tell Derek that he didn't belong there as Derek stood at attention. He told Derek that he should leave the academy and that he would never make it as an officer. As Derek continued the story, I already knew what he would do next. He asked the cadre for permission to speak. When it was granted, he told the cadre that he could do whatever he wanted to him. That he could throw his clothes out in the hall every night if that was the best he could do. He said, "Sir, nobody has worked harder to get here than me, and you can bring on whatever you have, but I am here to stay."

The harassment continued and there were many sleepless nights of picking up his room for inspection followed by trying to get all of his studies completed for the next day. We had talked so many times about how each experience has a lesson attached to it. When I asked Derek what he had learned from this particular cadre, he replied, "I have learned that I will never be that kind of cadre." As always, he was good to his word.

> *Logan, I wanted to take a moment and share with you a few of my memories of your Dad. They aren't of his many great accomplishments but of the little things that I remember most about Derek from the summer of 1999. I met Derek at the Air Force Academy the summer before his Junior year. I was a freshman going into squadron 36 which is where he had been his first two years, so he was one of the cadre or trainers for the basic training flight I was in. We (being the other basic trainees in D-flight going into sq36) dreaded Cadet Argels outdoor training sessions. We worked until our limbs were about to fall off and*

*then he would work on abs, back and neck. We typically just did pushups and leg lifts but not with Cadet Argel, he made sure we hurt from head to toe. But he never degraded us, just motivated us to keep going, to never give up.*

*Derek and I had lunch together a couple of times a week during basic training. Not that we were allowed to carry on any sort of conversation. He was an upperclassmen and as a basic trainee I had to sit at attention, chew my food seven times and not talk unless I was asked a question. As basics it was our job to get drinks for our trainers and Derek's favorite was pink lemonade. He always wanted one water and one pink lemonade. One day I was sitting next to Derek and he noticed I was not drinking my water and he asked why. I told him there was a worm in my glass. I was fully expecting to be told to drink it anyhow and I was prepared to do so. That's when I realized Derek was different than most of the trainers. Instead of enjoying the power and authority that he had and telling me to drink it anyhow, he simply picked up his glass of water and handed it to me. (that was the type of selfless act that I'm sure he did every day of his life and never even realized it) Then he took my glass and asked where the worm was (it was really small so I had to point it out) he laughed and said "how did you even see that little thing?" As a basic we weren't allowed to smile or have any sort of facial expression and it was so hard not to smile when he laughed with that big grin of his. There was another day at lunch they gave us a power bar, and we were only allowed 7 chews at a time, and those power bars are pretty tough and chewy. Some of us were taking little mouse size bites and others were trying to basically swallow it whole. Derek finally said, "That's enough, just eat the power bar, I don't care how many chews it takes." Derek paid attention to things that were going on around him and he took care of us.*

*One of the guys in our flight quit basic training. That night our flight was split up in groups of five for mentoring time. Derek was the mentor of the group I was in. He talked to us for about 20 minutes about how hard he worked to get into the Academy and his two years of prep school. He told us about how important defending our freedom was to him. I don't remember all of his words that night but the passion he had for his country and his beliefs I will never forget. The Academy didn't always make sense and did some pretty ridiculous things but Derek never seemed to be bothered by it, nothing tarnished that passion he had to serve.*

*A few days later my foot started bothering me. I didn't want to go to the doctors and be pulled out of training or limited on the training I was allowed to do. So I asked Derek if there was any way I could get ice. He said he would take care of it, and after dinner when I returned to my room there was a bag of ice in my sink. There was another on the day next, and the day next and the day next. I ended up having to have surgery after training, but I made it through training. I was very grateful not just because he brought me ice but knowing he would take care of us. In the military it means so much to have a commander or instructor like Derek, that you trust and can go to if there is a problem.*

*There were an odd number of females in our flight so I had to room with someone down a different hall. We were typically woken up by the cadre screaming and telling us what uniform we had to be in. My roommate's flight was usually in a different uniform than my flight. Derek would come down to the hall I was in and yell out the uniform for D flight, but one afternoon Derek was downstairs waiting for us to go on a run. Originally we were supposed to take our web belt and canteen but that changed and none of the other cadre came down my hall to tell me. So when*

*I got downstairs I got yelled at by a different cadre member for having my web belt when nobody else did. Derek came up to me afterward and asked me for my web belt. Temporarily forgetting that I was never allowed to argue with an upperclassman I said that's ok, I've got it. Then with a huge grin on his face but a very stern tone in his voice he said, "Give Me The Web Belt." At which point I quickly handed him the web belt and said, "Thank you Sir." He ran with the web belt and canteen around his shoulder the rest of the morning.*

*Logan, with all of your Dad's accomplishments it must seem like you have some pretty big shoes to fill; but from what I knew of your Dad what mattered most to him was that you love your Mom and give life everything you've got. Logan, your Dad was a great swimmer, water polo player, cadet and soldier . . . but the reason you dad is remembered so much by so many is because he was an extraordinary man (not just an extraordinary athlete) and extraordinary people, like your father, impact the lives of others even if they've only known them for a short time.*

*Logan, my hopes and prayers will always be with you. Jamie USAFA, Class of 2003 August 2006*

This story from Jamie is one of my favorites. Jamie was stationed on Vandenberg at the time. She came to the house one day with a friend for some wine and a visit. At first, I couldn't make her connection with Derek as she had graduated the Academy two years later. The two women came to back several nights later and insisted on making dinner for Todd and I. While she was cooking, she told us this story and we all laughed until we cried. I explained to Jamie that this story was so much like Derek. He would have insisted on making sure that everyone had water as he had been dehydrated during a couple of exercises. One of these incidents put him in the hospital. The other that was so true of Derek is that even as a little boy, he anaylized everything. While she told the story, I could picture him straining to see the tiny worm in the glass and questioning Jamie about her keen eyesight to notice this while focusing on her bites. I'm sure he was asking himself why he didn't notice this, and making a mental note to be more focused himself. Everything was a lesson to him and everything constituted some sort of training tool.

During all of his schooling, Derek would often ask me what I thought of his papers and his ideas for them. He would do a run through of what he was thinking about turning in. I came across one of these papers from the Academy that really illustrates his focus and drive to understand his motivation. It is one he shared with me and I have read it many times since 2005.

**December 9, 2000**

**I think I Can? No Wait, I Know I Can!**

**It was 0100 on Friday morning. The Instructor pulled us out of the water and said, "I don't think the water is cold enough. I want you to remove your blouses and your shirts." We took our blouses and shirts off and awaited the next command. The instructor then said, "About-hase, link arms, forward harch." It was at this moment I knew that nobody could motivate me. It was then that I realized that motivation comes from within. Sure people can pump you up. Like a coach they can say and do things to try and motivate you, but in the end, motivation comes from within. I was at mini-BUD/S this summer, which is officer selection for BUD/S training. I realized as I was taking a beating that you couldn't do things for others. I realized that no person could motivate you to do something. People can give you momentum to help you carry on, but motivation is purely an internal desire to achieve.**

Motivation helps us aspire to do many things. It drives us to excel in sports, school, relationships, and life. There are many aspects to motivation in which people have studied. For my topic, I chose to analyze the traditional mode of the thinking of motivation and come up with my own hypothesis. I wanted to look outside the scope of the book because how easy is it to look at a definition and settle for exactly that. From the research I obtained it is easily seen that there are many variations as to how people view motivation. I look at motivation according to many aspects in our lives, such as sports and exercise. I looked at the two main categories of motivation. There is both intrinsic and extrinsic motivation, which helps people achieve their goals. I will argue that although extrinsic motivation is powerful, you cannot motivate someone that is not willing to be motivated. Intrinsic motivation is a desire to achieve from within and any person that is willing to push him or herself has this desire. Sure a great speech or a great play will help give someone or a team momentum but motivation is all one's own.

When I think of motivation I often think of sports and how they interrelate. Sports can be broken down into three main categories. In sports you have a coach or coaches, a player or team, and the spectators, which include parents, friends, and fans. The coach is probably the most integral part of sports. He is the teacher and the student. He must learn to adapt to different players and their mental frame of mind. How important is the coach though? Is he really necessary for competition? How many times have you called up your friends and said, "Lets get a pick-up game of basketball going." When you finally get there, does someone say, "Can I be the coach?" So how much influence does a coach have.

I'm sure everyone has played for coaches with different personalities. There are coaches that are very vocal and there are coaches that are fairly quiet. Regardless, though, if a coach is vocal or not, do they motivate you? My water polo coach here at the Academy gets pretty fired up during games. I can tell that he is really into it because during the huddles he will get on one knee, dip his hand into the water and wet his lips. He does this when games are close and he wants us to pick up the intensity. He tries to motivate us by being in a mentorship role, giving guidance, and words of wisdom. I would argue that all coaches fall into these categories. I read a book entitled, <u>The Winner Within</u> by Pat Riley. Pat Riley is a very well known and respected coach. In his book he talks much about what it takes to build an effective team. However, all of his formulas for building winning programs, which is not only sports, stems from a desire to achieve. If someone is not willing to put in the effort and sacrifice to win or to achieve, than that person is already lost. How can you motivate someone who is not willing to be motivated?

Pat Riley said:

The team on the court is the team of the moment. When the first string snaps, motivate the players you have, rather than moaning about the ones you don't have. You'll never rouse The Winner Within by making people feel they're only a fill-in for sidelined greatness. (47)

Pat Riley is right when he says that you should motivate others, but that is all people can do. You can try to motivate others, but it will be up to them whether or not they are willing to be motivated.

What about a player in some sport that does not have someone else to try and motivate them? There are some sports where it is you vs. everyone else. Sure there will always be someone there rooting you on, but for the individual who is in a sport all their own, what keeps them motivated? Lets look at the wrestler. This is one of the best examples of an individual sport I can think of. When you are in practice, your best friend becomes your worst enemy because you are fighting for the one spot in your weight class. I remember when I wrestled in youth, when the buzzer went, I could not hear a word, all I could think of was my opponent and if he did this move what would I come back with. How about when a wrestler is down by 10 points with one minute to go, the only way for him to win at this point would be with a pin. **At this point nobody has any control over what you can or cannot do.** At this point someone could try to motivate you, but what they are really doing is trying to give you momentum to motivate yourself. How about team sports? There is a lot to be said about one player trying to get his team going. When a basketball player goes for a dunk is he trying to motivate his team? When a football player makes a great catch, or breaks free for a long run, is he trying to motivate his team? How about the soccer player that scores a header, is he trying to motivate his team? Sure, all of these instances can be thought of as motivating circumstances, however, perhaps these are more of a momentum tactics to get others to motivate themselves. What is the motivation for a team that is down by a lot with only minutes to play? It is an individual instinct to strive to play hard even when the outcome does not look well. Dr. Simons wrote an article published in the British Journal of Psychology. The article was entitled "Motivation Psychology." In his article he states that, **"Stimulating an individual's natural** curiosity will increase motivation." Dr. Simons article can be interpreted several ways, but he also talks about intrinsic motivation and he relates to a person's ability to motivate himself. His curiosity aspect in which a player questions his or her ability can be motivational. Players will view themselves in a certain way and question whether they can or cannot beat another team. George Shultz said, "The minute you start talking about what your're going to do if you lose, you have lost." A team or a player's ability to motivate them is based on how they view themselves. If they believe they can win, they will be that much more prepared mentally. If they question themselves then most often they think they will require someone else to motivate them.

Another powerful force which people misconstrue motivation for momentum is the spectator. Spectators have been around competitions since the dawn of games. In the movie Gladiator, Maximus was told if he won the crowd he would win his freedom. There is a lot to be said about spectators. In professional football, I'm always seeing commercials where the athletes are thanking the fans because they are what make the sport. How much can fans really make a difference? I broke spectators up into a few categories. Spectators include family, friends, and fans. All three have an impact on how the athlete will perform. I can recall a guy by the name of Joe. He was a phenomenal swimmer. I swam with him during youth but I was nowhere near the ability he had. I remember my mom came up to me at a swim meet and said "watch this." Joe had just finished his swim. He clearly beat everyone with ease. The next closest person was about half the pool behind. He looked back across the pool to where his dad was standing. His dad proceeded to give him a thumbs-down. I was dumbfounded as was my mom. My mom never pushed me into anything. I didn't have to swim and although I was never good, my mom had nothing but encouragement to give me. All I could think was where was his motivation to continue swimming? If his parents were not going to give it to him, it must have come from within.

So what kind of person is someone that needs someone else to motivate them? I'm sure if you asked anybody playing a sport, "Do you need someone else to motivate you," everyone would say no. Using this question to analyze my project I also took a look at exercise and what motivates people to stay in shape or lose weight. Why is it that one fat person will lose weight and keep it off, whereas another fat person will start to lose weight and then complain about extenuating circumstances? It is usually a lack of willpower that keeps someone from motivating themselves. Even Richard Simmons says, "You must believe in yourself first and foremost, if you want to achieve your goals." People who complain about time, kids, their job, etc... have not prioritized their life or they just don't have the desire to motivate themselves. When I asked my mom about a time she was stubborn about losing weight she said, "I was looking at this for the wrong reasons. I didn't want to lose the weight for myself but because everyone else thought I should. I'm having fun with it now, because nobody is telling me I should, "I'm telling myself."

My mom had set a goal that was specifically for her and that's what keeps her motivated. Much of the research I found on motivation was attributed to goal orientation. Setting goals is a powerful form of motivation because it sets a pathway. When a team creates goals together, everyone on the team knows what direction everyone is going. Goals give guidance as to what needs to be done to achieve certain things. Dr. Barbara Moses wrote "6 Degrees to Motivation" and had this to say about the achievements in setting goals. "Understanding your own motivational profile can help you understand what is most important to you in a work setting." This can also be applied to team goal orientation. When everyone knows what everyone else wants, than it is easier to achieve those goals together.

In finding research for my topic I came across a few interesting studies that were done. I found them interesting because they didn't look at the normal sports motivation and goal setting cliché. No, what they did look at was a classroom setting and how a teacher's motivation affects the learning environment. Can someone else's motivation affect another person? Dr. Brian Patrick wrote an article entitled, "What's Everybody So Excited About?: The effects of teacher enthusiasm on student intrinsic motivation and vitality." In this study Dr. Patrick went to visit several classrooms of students that ranged from grade school to college. He asked many questions of the students to include what kind of effect did they think the teacher had on them. Dr. Patrick concluded that enthusiasm was the most powerful unique predictor of students' intrinsic motivation and vitality. In the class a teacher's enthusiasm has an effect on the students motivation for learning. If this is true, perhaps teachers should be tested to measure their motivation (enthusiasm) to teach (i.e. money or fun). I agree with Dr. Patrick that teachers can influence a student's willingness to learn, but we must also take a look at the student's motivation for learning. Some students will excel regardless of what environment you put them in. Other students may have trouble in certain learning environments and it takes a good teacher that wants to see them excel to get their drive going. In either case both students still are motivated from within. In both cases it is solely up to the student and their ability to be intrinsically motivated for whether they will succeed or fail.

I often believe that motivation and momentum get confused. I feel that coaches, teachers, family, friends and fans can provide momentum for people to find motivation within themselves. Using this piece of information I came up with **Argel's Core Competencies of Motivation.** There are three parts that make up the core of motivation: **Commitment, Confidence, and Heart.** I found that any time I needed motivation these were essential for being intrinsically motivated. **Motivation** is about being **committed**. Any person who has ever made the attempt to set and achieve a goal would understand that you will fail if you're not committed to it. To be committed you can never hold back and never leave anything behind. My coach used to always tell our team, that regardless of what the scoreboard says at the end of the game if you know you didn't leave anything behind you have won. **Commitment isn't about winning or losing, it's about knowing you have given it your all.** Confidence is another key ingredient to motivation. **You must be confident in what you want to achieve.** Our course textbook says never set goals that cannot be achieved. If someone set a goal for winning the lotto, they will most likely be disappointed. How can someone remain motivated without confidence? To be confident you must know your limitations and be willing to exceed them. I looked at the Navy SEALS for this piece of wisdom. With almost an 85% attrition rate you must know that your body can do unthinkable things. However, this only starts with an unquestionable mental fortitude. **The last core to motivation is Heart.** This is probably the most important because It really can encompass everything. For Heart, you must be **willing to make sacrifices**. Heart in essence is the desire to achieve. If you don't have heart you cannot win, because you are not willing to work. I took a look at Air Force athletics for this core competency. We have always been considered the underdog in athletics. We take more classes, we put in longer hours, and we put up with more tedious tasks on an everyday basis than most athletes at other colleges. So this motivation to beat teams that nobody else thinks we can comes from heart. We **work harder, practice harder, and play harder** and when the other team lets their guard down, we beat them harder than any other team would.

People that have a desire to achieve and to win will motivate him or herself from within. It is not only a character check, but also a gut check. **Do you take responsibility for your own actions**? Would you blame your performance on your team? Would you blame your performance on your fans? Any athlete would hesitate to blame their performance on someone else. If motivation were attributed to performance then why would someone say someone else motivates him or her? Motivation comes from within but other people can help you find your motivation. I believe this is momentum. I would argue that this is where people get confused. A coach, teammate, family member, or friend can try to motivate you, but what they are really doing is giving you momentum to help you find the motivation within yourself. If someone ever asks you the question, "Why are you doing this," or "What are you doing this for" what will you say? I would argue that most people would say, **"Because I want to."** Derek Argel

The paper Derek wrote above shows so much insight into his character and how he thought out his goals and how they would be achieved. One of the turning points in his life was watching the reaction of a father to his son after a successful swim that day at a meet. I recall our conversation on the way home. Derek was asking me for a word to describe what happened and we talked about the word vicariously. I told him it meant that someone else tried to share in another person's experience through imagination or sympathetic feelings. I laughed and told him that you usually saw this kind of thing at youth football games, but not usually at age group swim meets. He started from that point to look at his brother and coaches as trying to help him with his momentum, but that only he could provide his own motivation.

> *"There was D-bone and D-nuts . . . seemingly everyday there was a new D-something—not to mention the really creative ones that are better left in the locker room.*
>
> *Even though Derek had countless nick-names, he had even more friends. It is said that even the most talented athlete only becomes great when they learn to help others around them be better players. If this is true, then in the game of life Derek is a world champion . . . for we will forever be better "specimens" and the world a more D-licious place because we were blessed that Derek Mears Argel touched our lives."*
>
> *For those that did not know Derek personally, he graduated from Cabrillo HS in Lompoc CA (the same high school as my brothers and me) in 1995. He wanted badly to attend the Air Force Academy, but did not have the test scores to qualify. He attended Northwestern Prep School at his own expense to try and qualify for USAFA. He was only able to raise his academic profile enough to be admitted into the USAFA Prep School in 1996. After two years of P-School he achieved his goal of*

*receiving an appointment to USAFA and in the summer of 97 Derek entered with the class of 2001.*

*In Water Polo, Derek was a 4-year letterman and an All Conference selection in his senior year. In January of his senior year he tried out for the Boxing team. With only two months boxing experience, Derek made it all the way to the Wing Open Championship heavyweight bout, losing in a split decision. Despite his athletic accomplishments, Derek may have been most proud of earning a 3.5 GPA in his last semester as a cadet. After struggling through two years of P-School and being in and out of Academic Probation during his first few semesters, to finish his cadet career on the Dean's List was an incredible testimony to Derek's determination and perseverance. I'll remember Derek most for his undying spirit and his endless sense of humor and contagious laugh.*

*After graduation, Derek was a stand out during STO training—breaking many of the STO all-time records. He became legendary and the focus of an Airman Magazine article. Derek was so physically superior to his classmates, the STO cadre (who lovingly called him "Mr. Water Polo") eventually required him to carry a 30 pound tree stump with him at all times just to level the playing field with the other trainees. Derek was a highly respected Team Leader and considered one of the STO rising stars.*

*Derek was a great man, dedicated to serving his nation at the very tip of the spear.*

*Coach, Jeff Heidmous June 2005*

As I sit at my desk and write this, I can't help but smile. Someone sent me the program from the boxing match and a tape. My father boxed in the Marine Corps, and when I was a little girl he used to do his little boxing dance and tell me to try to throw a punch at him. After throwing a few jabs his way and listening to his instructions about "keeping my guard up", I would tell him that I was not too fond of boxing. It didn't make sense to me that two people would get in a ring together for the purpose of beating each other up. Derek knew I was not keen on boxing. Although we had a great and open relationship and dialog, he never told me about the boxing tournament. The program cover features him and his opponent, with Derek in the silver trunks. The Cadet Wing Open Boxing Championship was a very big deal. I could tell by thumbing through the program. The ring announcer arriving inside on a Harley, the roar of the crowd, cadets in their dress blues escorting people to their seats in the arena . . . . and your Dad.

With only two months of practice, he would fight the defending Wing Open heavyweight champion. In an interview he said, "I knew Lee was a great boxer. As soon as the bell sounded, I figured win or lose if my hand was up at the end, I was a winner." Derek lost on a 3-2 decision that was the closest bout of the night. Derek knew that the Air force boxing program is one of the strongest in the country, and the winner would go to Nationals. Although considered the underdog of that event, he told the interviewer that he wasn't thinking that way when he crawled through the ropes. He said he was thinking about his brother John, who would have been a great fighter if he could have had the chance at something like the Wing Open. "I've always tested myself," he said. "I'd never really boxed, never really taken a punch. I wanted to see what kind of character I have, something else to make me tougher." When I saw him a couple of months later, I said, "Son, did you break your nose again somehow?" It seemed to be off a little. I told him we should see a doctor to have it set straight again. He gave me that smile and with a little chuckle said, "Ma, if I wait awhile, someone will set it back for me in a game or something." He said, "Anyway, it's part of my story." I think back to that time and fully understand why Derek didn't tell me about boxing and the Wing Open. He knew that I would have been on a plane and in the audience. He probably knew that it would upset me and I would not have provided the "momentum" he talked about in his paper.

In the summer of 1997, Derek earned a slot in the AFA Prep School. It was a water polo slot, with no guarantee of an appointment. He was able to attend practice with the team, and thankfully travel to some tournaments with them. It was during parent's weekend of that year, that I first saw the Academy. When I drove through the gate in my rental car, I was immediately impressed. I was going to meet Derek at the pool and watch a practice. I was returning from a working trip in Fiji, with jet lag and was somewhat disoriented. After finding my way to the sports complex, and wandering around the maze for some time, some cadets led me to the pool deck. My first impression was that now we were far beyond the high school days. The pool was much larger and so were the athletes. Derek was in the water as I introduced myself to the other parents. I knew the coach Jeff Heidmous, immediately from Cabrillo high school, where I also attended. I noticed someone else that was helping to coach the team. He carried himself with confidence and calm, and you could tell by his physical shape that he did not "fly a desk" for the Air Force. When Derek took a break, he ran over to hug me and say, "It's really something isn't it?" I agreed, then questioned Derek who the other coach was. He said, "Oh, that is Spano. He has an incredible job." I agreed that Assistant Coach in this great program would be very special. He replied, "No ma . . . his other job."

*I took a two year break from being an AF Combat Controller and became the assistant USAFA water polo coach from 1996-1998 and met Cadet Derek Argel during that time period. He played the "2-meter" position as I did when I was a cadet at the Academy and as a result there was a slight kinship of sorts between us despite the fact that Derek was a much better athlete. He was custom built to play water polo with a 6'6" frame of muscle and a work ethic that made the Amish look lazy. When he was provoked during a UC Santa Cruz water polo game, in part because he was an Academy Cadet playing at a left wing liberal college, Derek handled the situation perfectly: he cold cocked the guy and a bench clearing brawl ensued. Despite some blood oozing from his nose it was clear that Derek was the victor. Although I was occupying a position that was responsible for orderly conduct, calm and supervision, deep down I cheered that kid on and beamed with pride afterwards. It was at that time that I knew Air Force Combat Control and special operations could use a guy like Derek and I spoke with him about becoming a Combat Controller. Again he was custom built for the job. A physical animal complemented with a cool head under pressure, Derek excelled in Combat Control training; an arduous 18 month program. I followed his progress and it was not long before his name became a synonym for excellence within a career field that contains the very best warriors our Nation has to offer. He is one of a small band of folk that have been bestowed with a special and rare makeup of qualities that our country looks for in time of crises: selfless individuals willing to go into harms way and do the missions that few volunteer for or could even accomplish. Derek is a patriot whose exceptional character sealed his fate and he will be always remembered. Spano, June 2005*

The Lord does provide miracles. We sometimes don't recognize them as such, then give thanks later for the blessings we have been bestowed. The day that I landed in Colorado Springs for my first parent's weekend, I was completely green about the activities and how many would descend on the area around the Academy. I didn't know anyone there and had no connections. Derek was busy and I'm sure he assumed that I had made arrangements for my stay. I enlisted some help at the airport tourism desk, only to be told that I would not be able to find a room anywhere near the Academy. I took a room that they found for me at the Doubletree in the downtown area of the Springs. I called my mother that night to tell her I had landed safely and that I was going to have to find another place to stay to insure my funds would last for the weekend. She said, "Why don't you call the Gobles?" Mark and Kay Goble had been part of our Marlin's swim family in Lompoc and also attended our church at home. It had slipped my mind that they were transferred with the Air Force to the Springs.

When I called Kay, she was both surprised and happy to find out that Derek was at the Prep School. Without hesitation, they invited me to stay at their home, which was just a few miles from the Academy. On the pool deck that first day, Derek was delighted at my news and could not wait to see the family. With my bags and Derek's overnight gear, we walked into a miracle that night. The family knew that I was a single parent, with Derek a long way from home and Johnny in school at the same time. Derek explained the Sponsor parents program to them. This is a program designed to give the cadets a break from school on designated nights and some weekends to allow them a "home away from home." After a long evening of visiting and catching up, the Gobles filled out the necessary paperwork to become Derek's sponsor parents. The finished basement in their home was a cadet's dream, and they soon welcomed other "stray" cadets without sponsor homes into theirs. Mark was a Colonel in the Air Force and Kay a school teacher. The children already knew Derek from swimming. The Goble's for the next five years would provide a loving home, family and the spiritual help he would need to make his dream come true.

> *We first met Derek when our children swam with him on the Lompoc Marlins Swim Team. Then we were Derek's sponsor family in Colorado Springs while he was at the AF Prep School and also for his four years at the AFA. Family is the key word. He became a part of our family—wrestling in our living room, falling asleep sitting up on the couch, and sharing meals together. He was a big brother to our children and a son to us. I remember driving him to the AFA for the first day and he was wearing a*

> *Navy Seal t-shirt! I remember delivering his huge birthday cake on deck during a water polo practice. We remember his smile, his determination and his friendly spirit. Derek will always hold a very special place in our hearts.*
>
> *Col (ret) Mark, Kay, Brandon and Brittany Goble*

The family soon acquired a sign that read, "Gobles Air Force Academy Bed and Breakfast." I can't credit them enough for the love, guidance and understanding they provided Derek through the good times and the tough times at the Academy.

During one of our visits, Derek explained that he was getting a number on the AFA polo team. He said that in a way . . . he was playing for two people. He explained that one of the cadets on the team had an accident and it was a miracle that he was alive. Derek described him as a good man that had some hard luck that could happen to anyone. He was to be #12, and would do his best to live up to his own expectations of himself and the man that had worn it before.

> *Ms. Argel,*
>
> *My name is Paul; I played water polo w/Derek at USAFA (I was 98/99). I wanted to take a moment to tell you that your son's been in my thoughts and prayers for the last several months. Especially in the last few days. I've remembered Derek often. Among other things, I remember Derek as a devoted young man who loved his country . . . but, perhaps more importantly, I remember Derek as a compassionate human being who was always willing to help someone in need. If you don't mind, I would like to share with you something that I have not shared with anyone . . .*

*In the summer of 1996, I rolled a truck when I was returning to USAFA to begin my junior year. In my accident, among other things, I suffered a brain injury and had to rehab a year before returning to USAFA. When I returned, I had many challenges... and water polo was just "one more thing." I played in season... and Derek wore "my number" (12). My heart and mind were not in the game... Coach (rightly) decided to cut me in 98... and I managed the team for my last year. Long story short, in my last couple years, I really felt that I didn't have any true "pals" on the team. More to the point, I felt like I didn't belong at all. Derek knew that... but he always treated me well. He knew that I was facing many of my own challenges and he always treated me with kindness and respect. Derek and I never discussed my feelings, but I have long been grateful for his kindness. I appreciated that then; I appreciate that now. Quite simply, ma'am... your son was a good man. Your son was a good man... and I am a better man for having known him.*

*I am proud to have worn Derek's number a couple years before he claimed it for himself. Derek and his family will remain in my thoughts and prayers for as long as I live. God bless you, Paul August 2007*

I am still in touch with Paul. His ability to share his feelings and this story with us reminded me of Derek. I am grateful to him for knowing how important this story would be to you Logan, and what he meant when he said that in a way, he wanted to be playing for two people.

There wasn't much free time at the Academy, but outside the water polo family and his academics, Derek made two lasting friendships. On time off and trips home, K, Dustin and Derek spent the time they could together.

*Logan,*

*Your grandmother has been asking me to write you a letter since the day your father died. I never told her or your mother why I couldn't write the letter, but for me writing this letter means that your Dad is not coming back and it's really something that I've never come to grips with.*

*First, let me tell you that your mother is an amazing woman. Make sure you listen to her and obey her. Your dad would have nothing less. I remember the first time I met your mother, I knew she was perfect for your Dad. Your dad, as always, was indecisive about their relationship and where he wanted it to go. When I saw the way she dealt with your father, I knew she was the one and I told your Dad that. It was an honor to be in your parents wedding. It's been an honor to be your Godfather. I hope you know that in the future you can always come to me for anything.*

*I first met your father on June 26th, 1997. That was the day that we entered the Air Force Academy. Your father was not the best academically and had to go through two prep school to get in. I want you to remember that. It's a theme in your father's life. He may have not been the fastest, strongest, or smartest, but he worked the hardest and accomplished more than anyone ever thought he would have. Your dad was the tallest in our squadron, so he stood out. Since he had gone to the two prep schools he knew how to play the game and to get through things. He was the first one to show me how to be in the military.*

*From the first time that your father and I talked I knew we would be friends. He had a huge heart and was willing to help anyone get by. During our outdoor part of basic training, the recruited athletes always got picked on. There were about 6 of us and we all stuck together. Derek would always get himself into trouble to take the heat off someone else who couldn't run as fast or do as many pushups. One day he was getting beat pretty bad, and I jumped in to try to help him out. I remember when we were done, he came over and said thanks and I knew we would be friends forever.*

*During our freshman year I ate breakfast with your Dad every day and we hung out during our free time. Our seasons were during the same time, so when we had free time, it was at the same time. Your dad, Dustin Ireland, and I were inseparable our first two years at the Academy. We were always hanging out together. Your dad is the reason that I'm where I am today. I was thinking about quitting in the middle of my freshman year. Your dad walked in and just asked me how my day was going. I realized that I wanted to work and serve with people like your father, so I stayed.*

*During our recognition, your Dad and I were the only two athletes that weren't injured. I remember being on the Obstacle course just getting beat by Joe Kennedy. Joe was a great guy who your Dad and I both respected so we didn't mind him beating us. After about an hour I thought I was going to collapse from exhaustion. I remember your Dad grabbed my hand and held me through the last few minutes. I wouldn't have made it without your Dad.*

*You and your Dad are very similar. When I see you, I see him. Your smile is exactly the same. You have the same feet, and I think the biggest similarity I've seen so far is your dislike for being woken up in the middle of a nap. I remember I woke your Dad up one day because Dustin and I wanted to go to a movie. He threw his shoes at us (which were very large) and he had a few choice words for us. I never woke your Dad up again.*

*We spent every spring break together. Our freshman year we hit a deer in California on a road trip. Our junior year we tried to go on a cruise, but they wouldn't let us on. Our senior year they finally let us on the cruise. We also went snowboarding during Thanksgiving. We had a blast. I loved hanging out with your Dad. When you are older, we'll sit down and look through my pictures and I'll tell you about all our adventures. I'll tell you about the "I'm special today" plate that your Dad had to eat off of whenever he came to my mom's house.*

*Your dad's heart was huge. I remember I was having some family problems back home. I always confided in your Dad, so he always knew what was going on in my life. I remember that things were getting better. Your dad and I were sitting in a meeting talking about things. He knew that I was not happy. He bent down and gave me a hug and told me that things would get better. It was funny how he always had to bend down to hug me.*

*He was very modest too. I remember I flew to Florida one weekend to see him while he was in training. He was in Biloxi but was supposed to be coming home that weekend. His team got in trouble so he couldn't come home. He could only get an hour pass to leave base. I drove 4 hours early one Saturday morning to see him. We went out to lunch and I watched him eat 50 hot wings at Hooters. He told the waitress that he wanted 50 hot wings and she thought it was for the both of us. He had to call her back so I could order. We then went back to the base and he showed me his training area. I asked him how training was going. He told me it was okay and was explaining what they were doing. As I walked in the building I looked on the wall and saw that your Dad owned every single physical record. He owned all the swimming, running, pull ups, pushups, you name it and his name was next to it. Your dad would never tell me those things, but I always knew that he would do well.*

*Like I said earlier, your Dad worked harder than anyone else. People would always tell him that he couldn't do something. He loved to prove them wrong. I told him that he couldn't play soccer with us our senior year and he proved us all wrong. He played soccer with collegiate soccer players. He even scored a goal in his last game. Someone told him that he couldn't box. He proved them all wrong and lost in the finals. I fight that I think he really won. Your father was amazing. He even made the dean's list his last semester.*

*I can't even begin to describe to you all the things your father and I did together and the type of man he was. If there was anyone that I ever aspired to be it was your Dad. I was happy to call him my brother and he was a brother to me. He was the older brother that I never had. We went to Vegas, we went to Denver, we went bowling, we made road trips, we did so many things that I honestly can't remember them all. I look at my pictures every once and awhile and see your dad's goofy smile. The same smile I see on you.*

*Love Always, Your Godfather Kelii (K) March 2010*

I keep a picture in my guest bedroom of K, Dustin and Derek. It is a great shot of them laying on a snow bank on one of their ski trips during their years at the academy. The trio always took advantage of every adventure they could share in their free time.

*Dear Logan,*

*What can be said that hasn't been said already. Your Dad was an amazing man. I had the privilege/honor of spending my time at the academy with him. We went through basic training together and spent our first two years in the same squadron, sometimes as roommates. He had a powerful personality that few can match.*

*His body complimented his personality, big and powerful. Most of my memories are of him laughing and smiling. I spent every spring break with Derek and another good friend Kelii Chock who is also a great man. Both Derek and K were California boys and I grew up in Maine. On spring break we would jump in the car and start driving west. K always driving (sunglasses on), Derek always riding shotgun (seat all the way back) and me always in the back. I never got to ride shotgun simply because I was from the east coast and I think because Derek never would give up the front seat. We would drive nonstop until we got to Huntington Beach where we would spend a day at K's. Joann (K's mom) would feed us waffles nonstop and Derek and I would wrestle over the "special waffle plate." If I remember correctly it was K's birthday plate from when he was a kid. At some point we would pile back in the car and push off for Lompoc where we would spend a few days at your dad's home consuming tri tip (another California delicacy). Then, it would be back to reality and the challenges of life at the Academy.*

*We did this trip every year and from it I have many memories thanks to your Dad. We spent time in San Diego, Tijuana, Lompoc, and Huntington Beach visiting your dad's friends from high school and relaxing. I will never forget an image, forever burned into my mind. It's an image of your Dad with a garden hose somewhere near the Golden Gate Bridge hosing down K's car after we had what we thought was a near death experience. I believe it was our sophomore year and it was late. We'd been driving all day. I'm not sure why we were there, probably on our way up to someplace in Northern California. It doesn't matter. What does matter is that we had just crossed the Golden Gate bridge. K's little car was picking up speed and we were cruising on the Redwood Highway. It was dark but I can still see the deer as it lifted its head to see a Honda Accord bearing down on it. I remember the deer had no chance and neither did K have any chance to even touch the brakes. The deer disintegrated and your dad's laughter filled the car for the next few miles as we frantically looked for a place to pull over and assess the damage. Somewhere we found a lit gas station with a garden hose. I'll never forget us sitting at this gas station. K looking over his car, Derek still laughing while he cleaned what was left of the deer off the car. I can only imagine what anyone thought as they saw us.*

*Logan, your Dad had an uncanny way of making any bad situation manageable. He took life on full speed and for that he inspires me to be a better man/husband/father. His time here was short but his impact was immeasurable. Never forget that he lives on inside you and he is always there watching you, ready to listen, always smiling.*

*Dustin Ireland "Amtrak" February 2012*

In my note from Dustin he says he keeps constant reminders of Derek with him. In his office at Nellis, he keeps a framed copy of Derek's letter from 1988, "Why we should honor our Flag" with his picture in it. He keeps the Santa Barbara News Press article from June 11, 2005, "Salute to a Fallen Hero."

These trips with Dustin and K were cherished by Derek and a welcome change from the rigors of the Academy life and his schedule. The combination of class and homework, military training, etc., were combined with the practice and travel schedule of water polo. He loved it though and was at his best in the water and in the physical training.

The next letter is from Brent Reimer. He was a great friend of Derek's and a fellow water polo player. He shares a couple of funny memories from his recruiting trip to the Academy and what the cadets call, "Recognition."

## Recruiting Trip

*I first met Derek in the winter of 97. During my senior year of high school I took a recruiting trip to USAFA. Walking onto the Academy pool deck (which would become like a second home) during an Air Force off-season practice we would be introduced. My first impression was largely intimidation. Derek was already suited up and hoping to get in the water and was physically so much larger than me that I wondered for a second if I was really cut out for college ball. If you multiplied me 1.5 times I might have been his size. Derek was already friendly with most of the guys at the practice. He had lifted and been around practices enough thanks to the P-school. The Air Force players were finishing up w/coach and D was telling all the recruits that we could get in the pool for a bit. Some of the recruits were shy and probably didn't want to get in and feel insufficient at that point, but Derek just smiled at us as if to say, 'come on what else are you here for.' We all got in and eventually it was a '5 alive' challenge. Nobody started out taking it seriously but after Derek threw a few full speed burners past the rest of us, it was clear that some would graciously step out and some would try to step up. I did my best to remain cool but clearly got my juices going. I put two past D as keeper, this was clearly his weakness. But it wouldn't last and as it came down to the last two Derek burned me with a skip shot. After we were out of the pool, changed and walking to get some dinner, D said to me "we could be a pretty good team." That was just what I needed to find out for myself on this recruiting trip. This was going to be a good team. We would play quality water polo. Somehow you could just trust what Derek was saying.*

*Later during the visit all the recruits played some basketball together. Derek was a formidable and taller player to guard as we played but I had a few tricks on the basketball court. While I'm sure the basketball coach was by no means interested in us, we were off to another friendly but very competitive dual. I could sense that Derek and I had a lot in common, lots to prove and the drive to go do it. I started to understand what I most wanted out of a college water polo experience and Derek wanted the same things. It was the start of a friendship right there.*

*Thanks to Derek and Coach Heidmous, I made the best decision of my life.*

*Recognition weekend.*

*Freshman year was a tough time at the academy. The Water Polo team was clearly my highlight and saving grace. The light at the end of the tunnel is Recognition weekend and its one heck of a great thing to be done with, but quite the meat grinder to be in the middle of. I wasn't looking forward to it. It came nonetheless and once the hell started up and I switched on the adrenaline it became this huge challenge that I was ready to knock down with a sledgehammer. Everyone put on their tough face and charges head strong. I'd like to think that I was one of the toughest; I sure tried to be. One of the most vivid of all my memories however involves Derek. Somehow in the chaos of PT training on the way to Arnold Hall for a Giant Beat Down / Hoorah is that you all got a session with the entire class of 2001. Some of us polo boys grouped together going into the auditorium. We weren't in the same squadrons but we were as tight as anyone. When the beat down began, Derek somehow (and it really wasn't a surprise) got called out individually and at such a great time when we were the last row of seats in a group right in front center of the stage. Cadre were everywhere but Derek just earned four of his own. They descended to the aisle way directly behind us with all kinds of compliments. "Yes Sir, No Sir, No Excuse Sir" was the name of the game while attempting to 'rack it in' during high knees. The discussion finally broke down and Derek "got his rear over there and on the ground." I can never forget it because as he vaulted over the back of his seat into the aisle he smiled, the biggest goofiest smile that would of course get him lots of "special treatment." It was also the same smile that you'd see after you'd been laughing for half an hour straight. Derek was eating this stuff up. As his teammates we took a big gulp and hopped over the back of the seats to join him. Joe Kennedy caught me basically in mid-air and gave me the stay where you were. I think Charlie made it down for two or three pushups before getting pulled up by his belt and sent back to 'as you were.' I knew this bit from a basic training experience and everyone knew that D was in for it now. The Cadre worked Derek out until every single one of them was adequately astonished at his drive and determination. I recall that they had to force some liquids into him later that night and that clearly had this been any normal cadet, they'd have congratulated him and sent his prop and wings to the hospital where he'd be hydrating via IV. But this was Derek and everyone was getting another taste of why this guy was someone special and had that crazy twist to be the perfect Special Forces soldier. Of all the many wonderful smiles that Derek gave me during our time together, that one heading over the back of the chair will permanently be in my memory and always be at the top of my list of great smiles. Brent Reimer, January 2006*

Another great letter comes from a good friend of your dad's at the Academy. She is now a pilot and one of the most physically fit women I have ever met.

*This letter is probably the hardest thing I have personally ever had to do. I know that everyone who knew Derek knows what a great person he was, but I want to ensure that his son, Logan understands and knows how many lives his father touched, and what an outstanding person/officer/STO and most importantly friend his father was to so many people.*

*I first met Derek during basic. One could never forget his smile. When I first saw Logan, I chuckled at Logan's smile. It was most certainly reminiscent of Derek's smile. The same smile I vividly remember from freshman year. Mine and Derek's paths crossed so many times at the Academy. There are so many memories to recall, but for the most part I think Derek looked at me like a little sister. He always looked out for me. We had a bunch of mutual friends, Wendy O, was in his squadron and Wendy and I had grown up together doing gymnastics since age 4. Kelii and I became friends and is probably the person I keep in touch with most from school. Dustin and Aubrie, I could go on and on because Derek had a ton of friends. He was friendly to everyone, and had the personality that everyone liked to be around. He was funny, witty, and an all-around fun person to be around.*

*Derek and I had a little competition the 4 years at the Zoo (Academy). We had a bet that the one who has the highest PEA (Physical Education Average) of our whole class at the end of 4 years owed the other one dinner, we were sure it would be either him or me. So after every PE class and every PFT and AFT, we would compare averages, Mr. Heidmous instigated most of it and would give us updates. We were tied going into Senior year. I ended up breaking my foot second semester senior year and couldn't do the AFT. I can't remember what happened that D couldn't test, and another guy surpassed both of us. When Mr. Heidmous announced to us "the winner" we both just laughed and thought, well at least we don't owe the other one dinner.*

*I remember Derek (and Jeremy as well) would always "recruit" me to a bunch of different competition/challenges. I was the "secret weapon/token female." First of all they knew I wouldn't say NO, they knew I hated to lose, and that I would train just as hard as they would. Derek would push me so hard in training that I would threaten not to do another one, but he knew I wouldn't say no. He was certainly one of those people that I never wanted to disappoint. I thought so highly of him as a person, that I would never want him to think badly about me. I know the guys who* *worked for him in the military think the same thing. I remember Derek asked me one night if I would do the "Ranger Challenge" with his team because they needed a female. I agreed to it, not even knowing what it entailed. Our team is on the 5$^{th}$ or 6$^{th}$ event about 6 hours into this competition, doing this 9 mile 40lb ruck sack run, and I'm yelling at our team to keep up the pace that I don't want to lose, and Derek, just starts laughing. I ask him what the heck is so funny, and he starts laughing and making fun of all the guys on our team, because he's not even exhausted (no surprise here), and I'm the one yelling and him and I are dusting our team, and he can't stop making fun of the guys because they are getting beat by a girl. He always liked when I would show up other guys, but there's no way he would ever let me show him up. I think I might have beaten him in a racquetball game once, but then I had to drop the class because I missed over 5 of 10 classes due to volleyball and track. He gave me a bad time saying I got out of the class because I was scared he would annihilate me the next time we played in racquetball. When I first moved to Hurlburt, he even asked me to compete with his team for the "Fit Eagle" challenge. Every year when it comes around it makes me remember Derek.*

*I admired Derek from the time I met him. I thought he was invincible. I know that no matter what happened he would be able to take care of himself.*

*Logan, your father was admirable, he was highly thought of, everyone loved him, and they loved to be around him. His presence was overpowering, but he made everyone feel comfortable. He was awe-inspiring but personable. He was a great man, officer and friend. He will forever hold a place in not only my heart but everyone who knew him. Anna (July 2006)*

I may have mentioned that when Derek would come home for a visit, he could not sit still. He was really never at rest when he was anywhere, except, of course, in a deep sleep or taking a nap. In 2001, he was home for a visit. I turned around and he had his running shorts on. He said, "Ma, I'm going to run out to the base and work out." I tossed him the car keys. He got the huge grin on his face and shook his head up and down smiling as if to say yes, but he verbally said, "No, I said I was running to the base." I'm not sure what the mileage to Vandenberg is round trip from our house, maybe about 20 miles, but it was a distance. This letter talks about that running trip.

*Dearest Logan,*

*I met your father early in my Sophomore year at the Air Force Academy. He was attending the Prep School, and would occasionally practice and work out in our pool facility. Immediately I realized your Dad was someone special. He did not hesitate to introduce himself to everyone on the team, and I knew right away this was a man that was going to make an impact immediately when he joined the team as as a Freshman the next year. Well, your Dad did graduate the prep school and he joined the team in the Fall of 1997 when I was a Junior, and it was then that he and I began building a friendship.*

*Although I was a Junior when your Dad was a Freshman, he and I were the same age and it did not take long before I began to look up to your father. His work ethic, courage, and determination were unmatched, and competing along side of Derek Argel was always a privilege. When I did not perform well, I always felt like I let your Dad down, because he gave his heart and soul to every competitive minute he played in the pool, and I hated that his sacrifice was not rewarded with a victory. However, when we would win and I had a good game, a compliment from your father always meant the world to me, because he held high standards for himself and his teammates, and I knew if Derek*

*Argel gave me a pat on the back after a game or practice, I had accomplished something great.*

*As our time together passed at the Academy, your Dad and I developed a friendship away from the pool that continued well after he and I both graduated. I remember when your Dad and I celebrated our 21st birthdays in March of 1998, your Dad, Mark and I had to sneak out and celebrate because your Dad was still a Freshman. We had a wonderful time, and I felt a special bond with your father after that night. Over the years your Dad and I shared many laughs, and although staying in touch was not easy, it never seemed that he and I drifted apart.*

*The last memory I will leave with you Logan took place on June 2, 2001 at Vandenberg Air Force Base. This was the day I would be promoted from 2nd Lieutenant to 1st Lieutenant. Now, this is not a great milestone in one's military career. I think over 90% of Air Force Officers make this initial promotion; but nonetheless, I was excited about the new rank and of course the pay raise. However, my promotion ceremony was not something I was particularly looking forward to. I did not have friends in the local area, so I was going to have my boss and a random member of my squadron pin on my new rank during the ceremony. But, about ten minutes before the ceremony was to begin, your Dad waltzes into my office with his ear to ear super smile to surprise me. He had just graduated from the Academy, and was home in Lompoc on leave. It had been almost one year since I had last seen him and I shot out of my desk, shook his hand, and said "you wanna pin on my rank during my promotion?" Your Dad bellowed that perfect laugh we all know and love, and said "Robby you're crazy." Your poor Dad thought he had the upper hand when he surprised me that day, but I definitely had the last laugh. Of course he could not say "no" to me because he could see how proud I was to have him there as part of the ceremony. The photo of your father pinning on my rank, smiling, in his shorts, and t-shirt has always brought me a great deal of joy. I remember after he pinned on my rank, I reached over and hugged him—he made that a day special. Derek Argel, your Dad, was my friend.*

*Although your Dad was born with many gifts, what I will remember most about him was his kindness toward his fellow man. As you know, your Dad was a big guy, and because of his size he could have imposed his will on just about anyone. Ironically, your father was the kindest, most gentle person I will ever know. Just having known him has made me a better person, and I will always love him for that.*

*Logan, I wish I could bottle up all of the memories and experiences I shared with your father and give them to you. I have two children myself not much older than you, and one day when they are old enough to understand, I will tell them about my friend Derek Argel. On that day I will hold them close to my heart and say "Children, your Daddy has a hero in heaven . . .*

*Please know that your Dad is always proud of you, and that he loves you, your Mom, and your entire family very much. He will always be watching over you, and if you need to talk to him, I know your father will always be listening for his beloved son's prayers. God Bless, Rob October 2002*

*"Wendy and Derek's wedding in Florida"*

*"Derek deployed in Afghanistan"*

*"Fishing in Florida"*

*"Derek and Wendy at the squadron Christmas party"*

*"Passing time on the mini bike"*

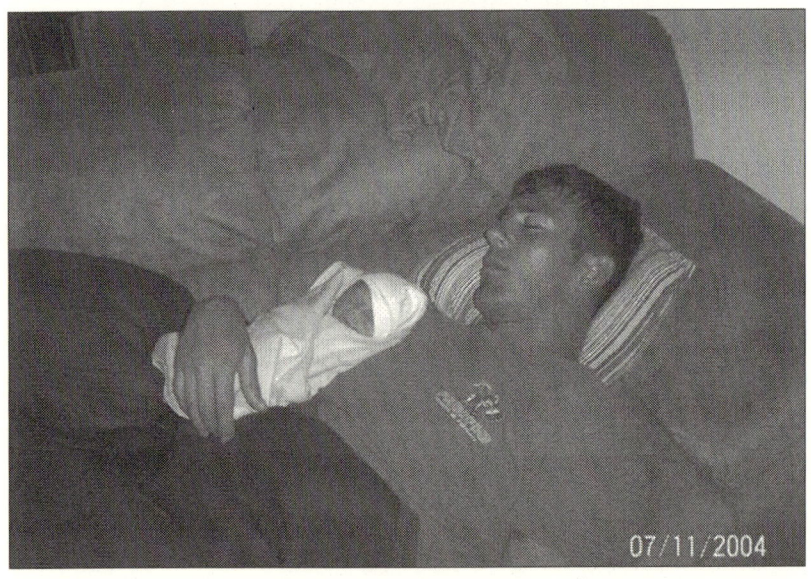

*"Derek and newborn Logan take a nap"*

*"Proud father"*

*"Derek on the beach wearing Logan's hat"*

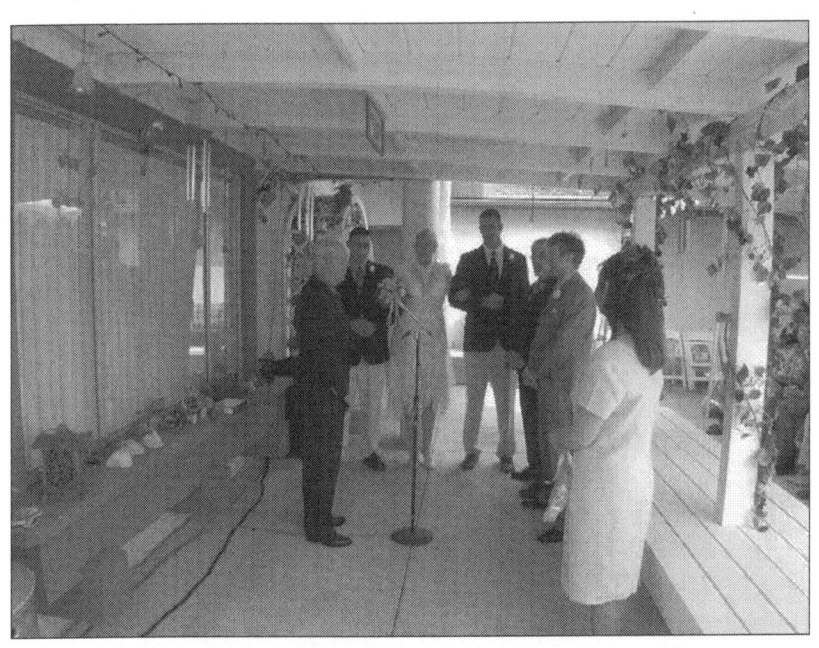

*"Johnny and Derek escorting Debbie to Todd down the aisle"*

*"Derek running with motor"*

*"2009, Wendy, Todd Allison and Logan our family grows"*

# Six

The following letter was written and verbally addressed by Derek to his team in 2002. It puts into perspective how he kept his promise having had the chance to try out. He was passionate about the men he worked with.

> "To coin an old adage, we've seen the best of times, we've seen the worst of times. However, I don't think we have begun to see what this extensive career field has in store for us. Team 06, you mark the beginning of a new era of soldier. First there, that others may live. These two phrases encapsulate a monumental job that you have only scratched the surface of. You have the ability to save and take lives by the thousands. Unlike our brethren SEALs, Rangers, and Special Forces alike, we train like no other to do a job which is unique worldwide. As I sit and ponder about the training that we've been through, the mental and physical pains, I can only imagine what war has in store for us. Will you remember the training you've been through, will you remember the guidance and wisdom that your brothers have bestowed upon you? We have been through highs and lows together,

but our one constant has been our ability to get the job done.

What other team has never failed an eval, what other team has passed their CDC's on the first try, what other team can truly say they have the camaraderie that the soldiers and brothers of team 06 have? I challenge any person to find another team out there that is more qualified to complete the mission than we are. We have seen a lot of good and bad times together since the beginning of the pipeline. I can recall unique stories that each of us has helped each other through, or at least had each other's back when it seemed as if nobody else cared. It started with orientation. Those two weeks of "we came out of Lackland for this?" Next was Air Traffic Control. I know the question in everyone's mind was "how can you possibly make something like this cool?" Well, as the not so distant future showed us, it was an intense sensation, feeling the blast of a C-17 as it roared to a screeching halt on a dirt strip. But that didn't come till later. For most everyone SERE (Survival, Evasion, Resistance, and Escape) came next, well the only memorable part for me was RT, you guys did the whole thing at once, but we all did agree that after it was all said and done, it was a good time. Next came Airborne, "Hoo-yah airborne" my ass. A 4 week school that could be completed in one. Well, we all bit our tongues with that one, or at least most of us did. Then came CCS and although we didn't all go through the same class, we all can relate to the trio. The thousands of push-ups, flutter kicks, and an assortment of exercises to make us feel like less than human. I'm still curious to know how a cartwheel will help you in combat. But alas, it was after this when Team 06 would be formed and the Saga began.

When team 06 was formed back in July of 2002, we weren't quite sure of what to expect. I'll tell you the most memorable mark hasn't been any physical beatings, it wasn't paperwork, or the BS that we have become accustom to. No, the most memorable part of the whole pipeline experience can probably be contributed to an individual. This man that I speak of stands a little over 5'5", but as far as the career field is concerned he towers over many. They could write an encyclopedia about his life, or if you were to record him talking on an average day, you would probably get the equivalent of a Harloquen romance novel. This man can go on and on talking about the glory days, and his stories never change. He can retell the same story 50 different ways and each one has a slightly different ending. Mr. John, our mentor, our brother, our friend. He joined our team in July of 2002 and has been with us ever since. I have to take a moment to recognize him because he has helped us become successful. John has been on me like stink on shit every since we came together to ensure the success of our team. It would be a disservice to the team if he wasn't recognized for our accomplishments.

However, so I do not digress too much, Team 06 joined for pre-scuba. Again we saw some highs and lows when our team was split during dive school. Injuries and illness split our team and for a time there was some thought our team wouldn't be able to maintain all our men. With sweat and determination though, we saw a tremendous success. We had 3 honor graduates, and two members on swim team one. A monumental achievement considering we are always a minority at CDQC. For those that may not know what it takes to get through this course, I can sum it up in one word: Fortitude. It's seeing individuals like John, Shaun, Ghram, and Ramses who I know don't like running but gave everything in their body, to not only show but prove they can do what their body may not want to. It was defining moments like this when I realized I'm surrounded by warriors and winners. Dive school would be the last time in our pipeline that we would have to prove ourselves to anyone outside our career field. From then on, it would be team accomplishments and team losses.

Through phase II, III, and IV our team has not always seen eye to eye. It's hard for people to agree on everything, actually it's damn near impossible. I know for a fact if I was surrounded by Argels, we definitely would have a hard time getting shit done. I could argue with myself for days on end, but that's why I'm glad we had such a diverse group of men. Sometimes it was tough for our team to get started on certain tasks because there were so many differing opinions, most of them right in their respective sense. So wrong, but as is such in a large group. However, when it came time for the mission, we were always locked on and ready to go. It truly is a testament to everyone on this team that no matter how much dissention there may have been between individuals, our own motivation that never faltered was that we wanted to complete the mission. Not just by the standards, no, we wanted to exceed them in every way. "Treat every scenario like it's real" this became a common quote of our resident Recon Marine Jason. We weren't out there to show the instructors that we could do the job, it was much deeper, we were out there to prove to each other that they could trust us to get our job done. We didn't want each other looking over our backs wondering if we were doing it right, we need that faith in our fellow soldier that while their back is turned they have full faith that we will complete the mission.

> **Team 06, you have missed two wars. Two wars that have already been written in the history books. Remember your training, your accomplishments, and each other. Remember some of the talks that we have had about integrity and your last name. Remember what the LT said about your last name, "It's yours, and you are the only person who can trash it." Remember that you represent yourself out there, and you represent your career field. You have been blessed to be a part of the select few that our career field has to offer. You will see combat, you will see death, and most of you will probably deal it. Take ease in knowing that your country, your friends, your family, your fellow controllers, and me, believe in what you can do, what you are capable of, and what you will do in the future. Hoo-yah team 06." (Derek, 2003)**

Derek's address to his team illustrates his enthusiasm, his drive and his complete love and trust for his team members with a little humor that all branches of the military dish out to each other. He had a great respect for who he called "Good Dudes" he worked alongside in all branches of the service.

> *Keesler AFB MS is the second stop in the Combat Control/ Special Tactics Officer pipeline. Here the students will learn Air Traffic Control (ATC) and go through a rigorous Physical Training (PT) program. A typical day for the student would start off with 10 hours of academics at the ATC School. After class they would move to the Combat Control Hanger and change into their PT clothes for 3 hours of tough physical training. After PT students would go back to the Locker House (barracks) shower, eat, and study. They would repeat this process for 3 ½ months. During this time they would be subject to academic and physical tests throughout their duration. As the Superintendent of the Combat Control Operator course it was my job to train the CCT students physically to meet the*

tough standards of the career field and to ensure that they met the academic needs of the course as well.

I'll never forget the first time I saw him. He was by far the tallest student ever to walk through the doors at our Hanger at Keesler AFB. I guessed he was an easy 6'6" clearly I would have to check for lightning before we went outside. I found out that Lt. Argel was an Academy grad and had played on the water polo team. I figured he would be strong in the water and have good endurance but I never would have imagined the numbers that he would put up on the first PT test. The PT test consisted of 3 calisthenics—pull ups, sit-ups, and push-ups, 3 mile run, and a 1500M swim. After crushing the Cals with 22 pull-ups/ 89 sit-ups/and 90 push-ups he put on a display at the run that I have never seen from such a huge human—a time of 16:29. I couldn't believe it out of the some 300 students that walked through those doors only about 5 could run under 17:00 and the other 4 were shorter than 6' and weighed 150lbs soaking wet, but this monster over 230lbs could plain out fly. When we got to the pool I knew that he would do well—my hypothesis was right he swam it in 22 and some change. At the end of each eval the events are graded and given a point value and compiled for a final score—the better you do on each event the more points you score. His overall score of the PT test was the best ever for an initial test and he improved on those scores over the next 3 evaluations. In the CCT gym at Keesler is a board that posts the top 3 records of the PT events for the past 10 years (when the board was made). Lt Argel's name is littered over that board with some of his records still standing today. Currently he still holds the #2 position on the 3 mile run with 16:18, #2 in the 1500M swim with 22:05, and most impressively is the coveted #1 of best overall PT eval of 1102 points.

The PT evals are one thing, but one of the most impressive things about Lt. Argel was what he was able to do day in and day out.

*For example—One of the first orders of business of each class is to go out and find a rock that will be carried by the team at all times when on duty. The purpose of the rock was to instill teamwork. The size of rock they chose was in the neighborhood of 16-20lbs (after instructor approval) it was painted and became part of the team's life for the next 3 ½ months. The rock is a great tool to develop teamwork during runs. Because of its size and weight it is impossible to run for any length of distance with it. During a normal 6 mile run the rock would change hands almost 100 times. As we started out on our first team run with this class the rock changed hands about 10 times. We were first introduced to the Argel factor—He could run with the rock the entire way without slowing him down, the team being good teammates would ask to help out and he would give it up, but after a short while it would end up back in his hands and he would again take his extended turn. After about 1 week we had to make a rule that we never made before—Lt. Argel could only carry the rock on a run when an instructor approved it.*

*Lt. Argel's team had three officers in it and we rotated between them as the class leader (to give all 3 officers the opportunity to lead). Lt. Argel was a natural leader. His class had its share of mediocre performers and he was determined to bring them to the high standard of the Combat Control demands. When these teammates could not keep up with the formation on faster runs he would assist them by putting his hand on their back and push them forward at the same time he would have 2 more teammates hanging on his shirt to maintain the pace. After a few weeks these students were able to maintain the pace on their own and ultimately have become successful Combat Controllers. As a going away gift to the school when they graduated the class donated the Lt. Argel shirt—it had been modified with handles on the back. Out of the some 22 plus students that I trained over my 3 years as an instructor, Lt. Argel was easily the most physically impressive that I have ever seen. Roger, June 2009*

In February of 2003, I was at work at my desk. Someone called me and alerted me to an article that had just come out in *Airman Magazine*. It was called "Mission Possible." I spoke with Derek later that evening. He said he was not happy about his picture being out there, with the job he was going to do. They were going to put him on the cover, but he politely asked that they didn't. It was an interesting article about the training for Combat Control. They talked about the tree stump that Derek would carry around to slow him down. I guess he had picked up a tree stump to replace the rock he carried at Keesler, to keep him more physically challenged.

> **"I don't know how they found out about the wood (here), but somehow here it is", he said. He told them that "Keeping mentally focused and learning to work in unison is the hardest part, because if you bring personal burdens to the pool, it affects everyone. Getting acclimated to the water is key, but right from the get-go you're getting kicked and you're forced to work as a team. We all have the same goals, and that makes it easy to help each other. Everyone is intent on getting through this course. After two years of being equipped with tools, we want to use them in the game. To be able to defend our country using our training would be unbelievable."**
> **Derek**

Although I am only beginning to understand the training and the brotherhood of the CCT (Combat Control Teams), I can say it is unique in this way. It is small and virtually not heard about in the general public. They are teams and squadrons. The friendships they form with the pilots and other branches in Spec Ops are lasting. Each depends on the other. This letter is from a mutual friend of your Dad and Dustin.

Dear Logan,

My name is MSgt (ret) FN. My call sign is PIMP. I'll tell you about the "call sign" story one day when you are 21 and we can have a beer together.

I was a combat controller from 1988-2011. I have been stationed in Europe twice, Hurlburt twice, Washington and Nevada. I have deployed into combat in just about every conflict from 9-11.

I met your Dad when I was stationed at 720 Special Tactics Group, Hurlburt Field FL back in 2003-2006 as the Joint Terminal Attack Control program manager.

At the group we had to stay current jumping and we'd often strap hang on some jump events at Advance Skills Training (AST). It was called AST back then and now called STTS where the pool is named after your Dad. Your dad was larger than life! You see, I'm a little guy so as I walked into AST for the first time to prepare for the jump and I saw such a large man (your Dad) I was impressed with the size and quality of men that were coming into the career field. This was my first impression of what the new training system was generating and it was impressive.

Another place I ran into your Dad quite a bit was on the PT field. We would either be doing Jungle Runs or better yet, playing Ultimate Football. I am very competitive and loved both, being on your dad's team or playing against him. Your dad was an amazing athlete!

I had the good fortune to go on a training trip with your Dad. This was January before he deployed for the last time. I was sent to New Jersey on a Close Air Support (CAS) trip to help evaluate some JTAC candidates for the up-coming deployment. I evaluated your Dad and I'll gladly tell you that he solved every tactical problem that I threw at him. Your dad passed this test with no problems. I was proud to sign him off as a qualified JTAC.

Your dad left that trip early to get home to take care of his team and his family. That was the last time I saw your Dad.

Your dad was a great man! I am much older and had more time as a CCT than him but I always looked up to him. He carried himself as a consummate leader! He led by example! No task was too difficult. He would be able to complete his tasks and help others with theirs. He fostered teamwork!!! Teamwork exuded from the pours in his body. Here's another story. One day we had a base wide run. The run was long and slow and became quite boring. Your dad with his deep, loud voice broke out into this song. Well, the song was very funny. Needless to say, it gave me new life on the run by making a boring event fun.

I was TDY to Nellis AFB when I found out about your Dad, Jeremy and Casey. That day as all days when we lose guys was very sad.

You have lots to be proud of! Your dad was on the fast track to becoming the leader of Special Tactics. He was that kind of guy!

There is more to this story . . .

I have had the opportunity to sing the national anthem at CCA (Combat Control Association) reunion dinners. I sang at the event after your dad's death. Your mom came up to me with tears in her eyes and told me she loved to hear me sing that song. That is one of the best things anyone has ever said to me and I remember it to this day like it was yesterday.

*My position as JTAC program manager afforded me the opportunity to work at the USAF Weapons School (USAFWS), Nellis AFB NV. I proved my worth to the Weapons School enough to where I got to move my family to Las Vegas and live at the school tasked with training Weapons Officers and JTACs alike. The 66th Weapons Squadron, (A-10 Hawgs) took me under their wing and made me part of their team. Logan, the USAF Weapons School is the most prestigious tactical, Air Power, institution in the Department of Defense. Only the best pilots and operators in the USAF get to attend the USAFWS. Often as I walked the hallowed halls of the school, instructors and students alike would know I was a CCT and come up to me and ask if I knew Derek Argel. One such man is now a great friend of mine named Dustin "Amtrak" Ireland. Amtrak went to the Zoo with your Dad and they were best mates. Amtrak is now an A-10 weapons officer and instructor at the school. I look up to Amtrak as I did your Dad. They both are cut from the exact same cloth ... a cloth of excellence, teamwork, humble, approachable, credible, real modern day Supermen. Amtrak, like your Dad, makes everything much, much better. I tell you about Amtrak because you have probably already met him and he will remain in your life for a long time to come. Amtrak has a tattoo on his back in memory of your Dad. That kind of love you don't find every day.*

*Your dad lives through Amtrak as he has taken the leadership role at the USAFWS to build a JTAC Graduate Level Program. This program will train CCT and TACP JTACs in the art of Air Power and how to instruct said Air Power to men in their units as well as advise senior leaders. This program is a benchmark for the JTAC community and will save lives while decimating the enemy for years to come.*

*Logan, this letter is long and it's long overdue. In closing, I encourage to take your father's lead and continue his excellence.*

> *Take care of your momma, love your family and friends and know that there is an entire community of Special Tactics warriors out there that are willing to lay their life down for you. God Speed little buddy! FN "PIMP" (February 2012)*

I was at the reunion dinner the night FN sang and it really was beautiful. I saw him again at the CCT mini-reunion in Las Vegas in 2011. Some of the guys came over to visit and have a couple of Irish Car Bombs with us. On that evening Wayne (a retired Combat Controller) told us he had just heard the news of the passing of Al Hooper, retired CCT and a wonderful man. I'm sure this was a first for the casino, but retired and active duty went to the floor of the casino to do memorial push-ups for Al. I have a picture of the Guarda with their money cart respectfully waiting to get across the casino floor until after the push-ups were finished.

There is a great photograph of some guys standing behind a C-130. They are standing with a sign that says "Wish I was at Coasters!" Coasters is a night club in Ft. Walton Beach just before you come to the Destin bridge. It was a well-known watering hole for the CCT guys. There used to be a large wall in the back with the green mean feet and most of the guys that came through would write their call names on it. I think that is where I had my first real encounter with Jack (FG). Linda Crate and I went in to see the little memorial Jack put up on one of the walls in the pool room. It had pictures of Jeremy, Casey and Derek, with a shot glass and beer glass with their initials on them. Sadly, it has been added to since that time. The wall also had another larger than life painting of the mean feet with the lightning bolt through it. I remember that Linda and I asked where they got the art for it. Jack was not at all embarrassed about showing us his own personal tattoo that was used as the model. We toasted the guys with a couple of Irish car bombs, which we found out were the drink of choice for the CCT at gatherings. I still keep the original copy of the poem Jack wrote down for me that day.

*"Here's to the men that wear the beret*
*Not blue, not black, not tan, not grey,*
*But the maroon and red that's on our head,*
*Like the men before us shed*
*May we all grow old together and never die,*
*So we can tell stories of why we f'n fly.*
*The blood, the sweat, the tears we give,*
*FIRST THERE, THAT OTHERS MAY LIVE."*
*-FG*

Logan, this is a quick story about how badass your daddy was. We were down in south Florida going through a training course and one of the things we had to do is to experience getting pepper sprayed. The instructors lined us up, 4 or 5 abreast. While eyes shut, the instructors sprayed, and we would immediately fall out of the formation in severe pain and suffering from the burn in our eyes. Most of us couldn't even open our eyes for about 10-15 minutes later, and the burn continued throughout the day.

Now when Derek stepped in to get his, the spray was applied . . . he paused, and then opened his eyes and said . . . I don't feel much, can you spray me again? The instructors were baffled, but agreed to reapply the spray. To our astonishment, once again he took it like a man, opened his eyes and said . . . let's do it one more time, but this time I'll have my eyes open. So they pepper sprayed Derek for a third time with his eyes wide open. At this point we all thought that he was absolutely nuts, so we watched in anticipation as he kept his eyes open after the application, and we could see he was in a lot of pain. Derek stood tall, with eyes open and just as red as I have ever seen, and as he made eye contact with the team . . . he yelled out an extremely loud . . . . Hoooooooooooyyyyyaaaaahhhhhh! And he was okay. FG, March 2012

We have met the most wonderful people at the CCT reunions. This letter comes from Derek's AST mentor.

> Deb and Todd,
>
> Met you at the CCA reunion last night. I'm John Thompson SMSgt CCT Ret. And current STTS CCT Instructor. As the class mentor for Derek's class I was with them every day in training while at AST and sometimes on weekends. These events come to mind:
>
> During PreSCUBA training all teams are shown how to run up boat motors and prep boats, then it's on them to do it right.
>
> LT Derek Argel's team had a hard morning of PT and pool training and then they had to get chow/prep boats and meet cadre for afternoon swim in SR Sound.
>
> When Derek and his Team showed up with Hummer/Boat/Trailer the motor did not work and we found out it had not been run up and was half apart. Team was told to go back to boat locker and get another motor. When they tried to use the Hummer, MSgt H told them they had to run back several miles across base with the motor and swap it out. Teams are normally given some type of extra training when attention to detail issues arise, as an ST Operator small things matter. As the leader and total stud Derek carried the motor on his shoulder. He passed a LTC pilot from AFSOC jogging and the LEC throws down his towel and starts walking. As I was following along behind the team (in a truck of course), I asked the LTC why he was so mad about the team for passing. I was told "What is the point in trying to exercise when I'm still going to get passed like I'm standing still by a guy with a motor on his shoulder?"

*Another time we had some issues with some underage drinking at the dorm, so our commander at the time ordered a curfew and all STOs and NCOs had to pull CQ at the dorm. Derek was at the dorm late one night and an SRA (not from our unit AST) had a room in our dorm. He just got back from deployment and comes back from 'clubbing' with a lady and runs into Derek at the entrance to the dorm. Well, let's just say I got a call at 2a.m. to resolve the situation.*

*Capt. Argel was an outstanding leader and had a caring for his men that is rarely seen. He was a physical stud on land and in the water and by far the most impressive I've ever seen.*

*John Thompson, SMSgt CCT Ret. GS-11 ST Instructor STTS October 2011*

This next letter comes from a dear friend of your dad's and of ours. He wrote this on his birthday last year, March 11 of 2011. He and your Dad shared the same birthday. It's a great story...

*Dear Logan,*

*I am hopeful that when you read this that in some way I am still involved in your life. I am Tony Travis, a combat controller who worked with and admired your father, Capt. Derek Argel. I first met your father when he was a 1$^{st}$ Lieutenant at the 23 STS. I had just returned from an overseas assignment in Mildenhall England (the 321 STS). I signed into the 23 STS and was given the honor of being the Blue Team Flight Superintendent. I reported in to Capt. Mason D. who was the Flight Commander to get my marching orders and expectations. This conversation lasted about 45 minutes where we went over ideas for managing the teams. One of the last topics we covered* *was a young Lieutenant that he wanted me to take under my wing and teach him everything I knew and help him master not only the operational side, but also the management side expected of our Special Tactics Officers.*

*Great, just what I needed, a wet behind the ears snot-nosed Lieutenant that I was going to have to babysit for who knows how long. Lieutenants are a tricky beast, they think they know everything and teaching them that they don't and more importantly that they need to solicit information from their enlisted force was usually like pulling teeth from a rhinoceros. Difficult to say the least. Capt. D took me over to his office to introduce me (the whole time I am thinking "what is this little kid going to look like and does he shave yet.") That was when I met the most intimidating man I have ever come across in my entire career, your father. Let me start this with the fact that I am not easily intimidated. While I am not the largest individual in the room on most occasions, I can handle myself fairly well and usually am the one doing the intimidating (at least in my mind). Not only was he one of the most physically intimidating individuals I have ever come across, but his entire mannerism exuded a calm confidence that you just can't teach to someone and is seldom, if ever, seen in someone that young. Usually it takes years of experience to get to that level. I believe your father was born with it, which is very rare indeed. Young Lieutenant Argel and I sat down and for the next two hours we talked about combat control, how to get the team ready for the next deployment, what can we as leaders be doing to make our men more successful, how can we manage the schedule to get them proficient but still balance time with their families. Again, this is coming from a young Lieutenant that is not supposed to know all the right things to be concerned with. Usually all they want to do is get trained and deploy themselves so they can check that box. It became immediately clear that his primary focus was on the care, welfare and moral of the men working for us. Could I see the* fire in his eyes, was it apparent that he wanted to prosecute the mission and deploy? Absolutely, but he understood that his job was to prepare his team and not focus on himself. That is what made him one of the finest young leaders and most respected young officers in our career field. He never put his personal desires ahead of his responsibilities and although he was a hard man and expected a lot from his men, he was just and fair. We ended that first conversation with a statement from your father that once again showed his maturity and ability to self-analyze his capabilities. "TT, until I get this s—down, I am going to be in your hip pocket, don't hesitate to pull me aside and correct me if I am doing something wrong." It was very seldom that I ever had to pull him aside and never because of a failure on his part. It was always something to do with Air Force instructions, their interpretations, or a requirement that needed to be accomplished to accurately document training or schedule a trip. Those kinds of things have to be learned and he learned rapidly.

I would like to be prideful and say I carried your father through the first year on the team, but the truth is he carried the team. Lee Iacocca, former CEO of General Motors once said "Lead, follow, or get the h—out of the way." I can absolutely guarantee your father never followed or got out of the way. He absolutely epitomized the qualities you look for in a leader, a man, a husband, a father, and a friend. While I provided your father some input to help him succeed, he was fully capable of succeeding on his own.

I am sure you have heard stories of how he single handedly carried a 55 HP engine so his team could compete, or how he was a phenomenal athlete always leading from the front etc . . . all those things were just a small part of who he was. The only time I ever saw softness on his part is what actually made him more of a man. The softness came from talking about his family, your mother Wendy and you Logan. I wish I had the writing *skills to capture the love and pride in his voice and eyes when we would speak about our families while working late or on some TDY waiting for the next flight. I just do not possess the skills to convey the emotion of the man, your father, who I am honored to have worked for and proud to call a friend. For that I am truly sorry.*

*I have several memories and stories of your father that I hope to someday be able to tell you. I would like to close with one that may not make any sense to you, but reminds me of the humor your father possessed. In this story he not only bested me, but also reminded me of where my focus needed to be, on the future.*

*We were on our first and only deployment together. I had moved up to the squadron superintendant position and he had become a Flight Commander. I had the opportunity to deploy to a firebase (where all of us wanted to be) and he was stuck on the first half of the rotation working in the Special Tactics Operation Center (where none of us wanted to be). We kept in contact on a daily basis and he would forward me updates, review my request etc . . . Late at night if I wasn't on patrol I would ping him every so often to rub it in that I was at a firebase living the dream while he was riding a desk. One night after coming off a three day patrol I sent him a picture looking out over the barrel of a 50 caliber machine gun on the back of a gun truck with the caption "this is your future." Very pleased with myself because I knew he wanted to be out with the guys and this picture was just rubbing it in, I eagerly awaited his response which I imagined to be something like "that's jacked up" or something along those lines. Instead he took a picture of a computer screen on a desk with a caption that said "this is your future." I sent him a reply that said "that's jacked up" and went off to bed wondering how my great little joke had backfired on me.*

*I often sit and stare at my blank computer screen when I come in to work in the morning and am reminded of that time. You see he was the only contact I had back to our guys while I was at the firebase and despite how busy he was, he always found time to send me updates or send messages back and forth on lonely nights to let me know he had my back. I will forever cherish those late night typed out conversations over satellite.*

*About a month later I came back in from a week out on patrol anticipating telling him all the cool stuff that was going on and trying to one up him. Instead I had a single message from our commander telling me we had lost three warriors, one of them being your father. I cried for a few hours, changed the batteries in my radios and went back to work. He wouldn't want me to neglect my duties. I have tried to honor him ever since by taking care of our Airmen like he did and not put my personal desires ahead of my responsibilities.*

*I hope this letter can give you some insight to the type of man your father was and will forever be. Please be proud of him and know that he loved you beyond the capabilities of words to explain. He is the standard I have held all other young officers to since and someone I am truly honored to have been my leader and friend. I write this letter to you on my birthday. I find it fitting that it is done so. Very respectfully: Tony "TT" Travis March 11, 2011*

This is a letter from your dad's Commander at the time. It is especially touching as the CCT Memorial he is speaking of is the one we visit each year, and where you have done so many push-ups with the team members.

*Deb Argel-Bastian*

*Logan,*

*Words to describe your Dad . . . extremely patriotic, loyal, passionate, energetic, disciplined, motivated, dedicated and caring.*

*Your father had once told me he felt he was destined for great things and if giving his life for his country was a part of it—so be it. He loved his country and was very passionate about it. He wanted to be in the action at all times and never wanted to be off the line and away from the fight. In fact—this was a very big concern for him and it gnawed at him. Being a Special Tactics Officer (STO) provides some field time for the young officer, but after awhile and the more rank a STO makes—the less time spent in the field with the men. Your father toiled over this at length—it really saddened him to think he would have to come off the line. In the end—what kept him in the Air Force and got him to take the assignment to Royal Air Force Mildenhall in England was his loyalty to his men. He felt he owed it to them to stay with them and to continue to be there for them.*

*I also want to share something I witnessed of your father that told a lot about his character. As a team—we were at the tail end of a run swim run physical training session and your Dad was naturally in the lead. I watched him run from the swimming pool back toward the squadron. This route took him by the "air park"—which is also home to our Combat Control Memorial. He had no idea I was behind him or that any one was behind him for that matter. I saw him quickly divert to the right and run down the street toward the Combat Control Memorial. He promptly stopped in front of it and dropped down and did push ups—a tradition to honor our fallen brethren. I recall thinking how impressive that was and that one selfless act said so much about your dad's character. Now it is your father that has sacrificed for us—his name now appears on the memorial that we honor. I will continue to drop down and do Memorial push-ups in honor of your father—just like he did for those that went before him.*

*I also recall a time just before we deployed in the winter of 2005 on a late dark evening in which your Dad stopped by my office to see me. It was very evident to me—your Dad was very ill. I asked him what the heck he was doing still here—especially so under the weather? He told me—he was helping one of his men and could not leave him to deal with the problem himself. This selfless act said a lot about your Dad—especially his loyalty. I recall being very impressed with him that very moment. He could have easily gone home under the guise of being sick, but instead he "sucked it up" and was there for his men. He always was there for his team. Your dad was very selfless.*

*Your dad had just pinned on the rank of "Captain" the day he died. I had written him a card in which I told him he had a very bright future—no matter what he did with it. Because you see—he was a winner in all walks of life who gave it his all in absolutely everything he did. He set the example for even older guys like me to follow. Your dad was "the best of the best." Brad October 2010*

I never really knew much about your dad's job, so I had many questions. I think it is best described by a letter you received early on. This letter was written on Father's Day of 2005.

*Dear Logan,*

*This letter is for you when you are old enough. It is a letter about your father, Captain Derek Argel. Your mother will give it to you or read it when it's time. It is so important that you know who your father was, what he did and what his life meant. There are many people who were very close to your father who will tell you all kinds of wonderful, funny and great things about him. I will tell you what I know about your Dad as his group commander—I will tell you about what your father did in the Air Force.*

*Logan, your Daddy was a wonderful man who lived life to the fullest. He had a love for living that was wonderful to see. Your Dad always tried his best, did his best, and lived his best. Your Mother and many others will tell you about his growing up years, his time in high school, at the Air Force Academy and more. These things led to him joining the Air Force and serving his country as an Air Force Special Tactics Officer. I am also a Special Tactics Officer and I met your Dad early in his time in the Air Force. I spent time with him overseas in the war zone and back home here in the United States. I watched him excel in everything he did. He was an amazing man.*

*What's a Special Tactics Officer? As a Special Tactics Officer (or STO for short,) your Dad was among the most elite combat leaders in the entire military. As a STO, he led other elite fighting men in Special Tactics including combat controllers, pararescuemen and mission support groups. Your Dad planned and led important special operations missions like parachuting out of airplanes, scuba diving in the ocean and sneaking around at night like a Ninja so the bad guys couldn't find him or his team. Also as a STO, your Dad was an expert at talking to airplanes by radio from the ground and guiding them into a target so they could drop on the enemy. He also knew how to guide airplanes in to land on dirt airstrips nearby and how to lead a team to rescue Americans in trouble. He had a whole lot of really cool skills like shooting, rock climbing, swimming, scuba diving, rappelling, skydiving, (and a whole lot more) . . . and he was really good at them.*

*How did your Dad get to be a Special Tactics Officer? There are only a certain number of STOs in the whole Air Force, and so we handpick each one from the top candidates who apply. Of the hundreds that want to be Special Tactics Officers, only a few each year get selected to start our training. Fewer make it through our two years of training to wear the Red Beret like your Dad did. Your Dad applied to become a STO while he was a cadet at the Air Force Academy. His application package looked really good, so we chose him to come to our weeklong assessment course at Hurlburt Field. This week was hard-filled with running, exercises, marching and lots of stress. We put pressure on all the applicants to see what they were made of and so we could choose the best ones. Well, your Dad did great at this assessment and so we picked him to start our training . . . which is some of the toughest training in the world that we call "The Pipeline."*

*How did your Dad do in the Pipeline? Logan, you know by now that your Dad was quite an athlete. Well it showed because he did great during the Pipeline. He was strong in body, strong in his mind and strong in his heart. He set records (especially in swimming) and helped other trainees to get through the training. We could see even back in 2002 and 2003 when he was a trainee, that he was a special officer and a special man. During the pipeline, your Dad trained to do a whole lot of things . . . including: static-line parachuting, military freefall parachuting, combat scuba diver, land survival training, water survival training, Air Traffic Control, Terminal Attack Control (that's where we guide in airplanes while we're on the ground to drop on the enemy.) At Combat Control School your Dad leaned how to sneak around in the woods, shoot his weapons, set up aircraft landing zones, operate radios, and how to guide aircraft for safe landings and takeoffs (using his radio on the ground.) He also practiced taking over an enemy airfield by force and leading "Combat Search and Rescue" missions to save people who are in trouble. Like I said, your Dad did great in training—he was one of our best ever. And he really had a good time doing all these cool things . . . well, most of the time . . . sometimes the training was so hard that nobody had a good time. But your Dad always did his best to help his teammates . . . that's why we all loved him. He was one of our best trainees ever. The best thing that happened to your Dad during the training Pipeline is that he met your wonderful Mom. Then, after training, they got married in Fort Walton Beach . . . and then you were born, which made your Dad and Mom really happy.*

*What did your Dad do after the training Pipeline? When the Pipeline was finally over, your Dad was assigned to the 23$^{rd}$ Special Tactics Squadron (or 23 STS for short) at Hurlburt Field in Ft. Walton Beach, Florida. In Special Tactics we have __ squadrons of people that are stationed all over the world. The 23$^{rd}$ Special Tactics Squadron is our __ biggest squadron and is very important to us. Your Dad started out as the assistant Team Leader on Blue Team, one of the __ teams at the 23 STS. Even though he was new, he learned everything quickly and was a real leader. He was very good at all of his skills, always helped his teammates, and knew how to get things done right. He helped to plan and lead his team on advanced training including martial arts fighting, combat shooting, combat diving, sneaking around techniques, and how to fight as a team. Because he was so good in the water and a great scuba diver, he was selected to be the Diving Officer for his squadron, the 23 STS. He was also selected to go to a special US Marine School and got really good at guiding in airplanes to the target. I said earlier that he was a good leader. Well, during Hurricane Ivan, which was a huge storm that hit Ft Walton Beach area in September 2004, your Dad volunteered to lead our six-man "stay-behind" team. The stay-behind team's job was to help open back up Hurlburt Field after the storm wrecked the base. He also volunteered to help people outside the base whose homes had been smashed up. For his leadership and teamwork, we awarded him with an Air Force Achievement Medal.*

*After your Dad had been on Silver Team for a while as assistant team leader, his squadron commander selected him to become the team leader of Red Team. This was around December of 2004. This was a really special job because Red Team is our team of pararescueman (or PJs for short.) After your Dad took over, he trained hard with Red Team at rescuing people and saving their lives—especially in combat. Your Dad trained his team so they could rescue anyone anywhere—in the ocean, in the mountains, in the jungle, in the desert . . . anywhere. During this whole time, your Dad was getting ready. Getting himself ready, and getting his team ready for deployment—deployment over to the war zone to fight in the War on Terrorism.*

*Sincerely, "RZ" June 2005*

One of your dad's great friends wrote a wonderful letter on July 18 of 2005. I was so happy to be able to include this letter. I can't imagine how difficult it was to write. When we got the tape from the service for the guys in Afghanistan, he spoke about your Dad. The following is his letter:

*Wendy and Logan-*

*It is with great sadness that I write this letter to you. It has only been 50 days since I lost Derek, Jeremy, and Casey—but in the short time I had to spend with each of them, they touched my life, and with this letter I will try to convey in words the profound impact that Derek had in my life.*

*I met Derek on June 23, 2001, on the first day of the Special Tactics Officer tryouts, only one month after I put on Captain myself and only days after my son Bailey was born. We were both part of a strong team of men hand picked to tryout for this noble profession. My first impresssions were of a man larger than life. Not only in stature but in presence. When Derek spoke,* he commanded attention not only through his words but also in his charisma and poise. The aura around him was instantly recognizable. When Derek had something to say, everyone listened. With him by my side through our selection program, our team was strong and our success was unheralded—we ended up with six selectees including Derek and myself.

His endless capability and talent never ceased to amaze me. As Derek powered through the combat control training pipeline, he left a warriors impression. Record books were re-written. Traditional officer roles and responsibilities were shattered as Derek took on multiple task of team leader, motivator, manager and disciplinarian.

One specific event in our pipeline together stands out when we conducted a "monster mash." This competitive event among teams is similar to an adventure race with combat control specific task at multiple stations located throughout the local area. This one is particular, on a hot September morning in 2003, started off with teams dropped off on Okaloosa Island and making their way back to base with a 40 pound rucksack, ½ mile of water, and 8 miles of land in between. With less than two miles left each team was given an outboard 40 horsepower engine, weighing nearly 200 pounds, to carry to the finish. When my team and Derek's team were within 200 meters of the finish, neck and neck, I observed a feat of such magnitude it still boggles me today. Derek, wanting his team to win, took the engine out of the team's combined hands, onto his shoulders, and ran to the finish with the engine to ensure his team finished before mine. I still enjoy telling that story to friends and co-workers alike. That is the kind of man Derek was—he would carry the entire weight of the team to finish. A competitive spirit unlike any other.

You can imagine my pleasure when I completed the pipeline and was assigned to the mighty 23$^{rd}$ Special Tactics Squadron, *along with Derek. For the past two years I worked hand in hand with him in countless projects, missions, and late evening talks after everyone else had left—always vying to make things better for his men that he loved and the profession he represented. I remember our first deployment together, and his excitement in taking men on countless missions and serving at the "tip of the spear." The smile on his face was priceless.*

*On this summer's rotation, I was given the honor for my first squadron command. It gave me comfort that Derek was my right hand man—and when I left the operations center for whatever reason, typically late at night after an exhausting day, I left it in Derek's command. And with that I rested soundly knowing our men couldn't be in better hands. Derek also set precedence while he worked with me. Not only for his sound judgment and wealth of skill, but for the mission sets he took part in. He continued to blur the line between enlisted and officer positions. Our countless late night discussions will be cherished for the rest of my life. There is not another person I would have rather had by my side.*

*For Wendy—know that your strength and determination have had quite an effect on me. Only since our team returned from the deployment is his loss now becoming a reality to me. I didn't know how to handle it, but I see you and it gives me strength to continue on, to make Derek proud of us still, and for me to be a better man. Thank you for your strength in all that you do.*

*For Logan—I only wish you could know your father as I did. Words on paper don't do justice to his presence, love, caring, strength, and humor. I will never forget him and the impact he left on my life. Stand tall and proud knowing your father defined the meaning of love for your family and the nation he served. He was my teammate, but more, he was my friend.*

*The strongest words I can think of that remind me of Derek are passion, determination and enthusiasm. For life, for his men, for his family. I only hope I can be half the leader he was. There is an empty space in my soul without Derek here beside me, but I know he is watching over us and we often still discuss my dilemmas at work just like we did in Bagram, Afghanistan this summer. With that, I would like to recall a quote I used at his memorial service at Bagram. It sums up the kind of man Derek was.*

*"It is not the critic who counts, not the man who points out how the strong man stumbled, or where the doer of deeds could have done better. The credit belongs to the man who is actually in the arena; whose face is marred by the dust and sweat and blood; who strives valiantly; who errs and comes short again and again; who knows the great enthusiasm, the great devotions and spends himself in a worthy course; who at the best, knows in the end the triumph of high achievement, and who, at worst, if he fails, at least fails while daring greatly; so that his place shall never be with those cold and timid souls who know neither victory or defeat. (Teddy Roosevelt) "Sincerely, "SF" July 2005*

# Seven

Early in June of 2005, I was beginning to file some of the stories in some order. I asked Wendy and Mike and Jane Wild (Logan's grandparents) to write down some of the memories of Derek they had shared with me. I'll begin with the great letter of how Wendy and Derek met.

> *It was March 2002, St. Patrick's Day. My friend and I were out for the night to have drinks and chat. We were sitting at the bar of an Irish pub when she turned and said to me, "Look at that tall guy over there." I looked over my shoulder to see the most gorgeous man I had ever seen. Needless to say he stood out amongst everyone and little did I know that this man would be the love of my life, my future hubby and best friend.*
>
> *Derek and the buddies he was with were trying to make their way to the bar. The only available space to stand happened to be directly behind us. Of course I was too shy to say anything to Derek then but my friend and I did manage to hear the guys order car bombs, have a couple jokes and then be on their way. I didn't think I would see him again.*

*After a couple of beers, we decided to head across the street to a local bar named, AJ's. When we walked up the stairs I was amazed to catch eye with the tall guy from the Irish bar. This is the first time Derek and I actually looked at each other face to face. My friend and I would do a round around the bar and then Derek and his buddy would do the same. Each time we would look at each other until finally his buddy came up to us and introduced himself. It took a second for Derek to say anything so I turned to him, looked up and said, "Hi, I'm Wendy." He said, "Hi, I'm Derek." We sparked instantly.*

*We spent the whole night talking. We found out that we had a lot in common and even had some mutual friends. As the conversation went he must have been trying to impress me because he mentioned that his mom used to work at Sea World. I'm sure by the excitement on my face he knew he was impressing me, I had mentioned earlier that I was into that kind of work!*

*We had an amazing night talking and getting to know each other. We even took a walk on the docks by the water. We saw this huge boat that was for chartering cruises and Derek looked at me and said, "You want to climb aboard? We climbed all over the boat and snuck off before anyone noticed.*

*As the night ended he got my phone number and we said our sweet good-bye's for then. I was smiling all the way home. When I got to my house, on my answering machine there was a message from Derek. He sited some romantic verse from a poem. It was cheesy but perfect. We spent the entire two next weeks together before he headed off to CCT school up in N.C.*

*Wendy, June, 2005*

What Wendy didn't know that evening was that Derek made about six calls to me that night. He would excuse himself to go to the bathroom or something and make a call to me. He said he was calling for "back up." He told me that he had met a wonderful southern girl, and that his buddies were not helping him much. They were telling her things to impress her like, "This guy (pointing to Derek) can kill people with his bare hands." Not exactly the lines you would use on a first introduction. He wanted to know first the years I was at Sea World, next call about the Houston Zoo, the Miami Zoo, etc. During the first call, I misunderstood him and said, "What about your training?" He said, "Ma, I'm not trained for this!" He told me that she was definitely the one, and this was love at first sight. He told me that she smiled from the inside out . . . she was genuine and that her laughter and smile were from the soul.

> In Aug 03, Derek graduated from his 2 year combat controller special tactics school. Wendy had been dating Derek for some time now 1 or 1 ½ years, and it was pretty evident that Wendy was serious about him. Jane and I were getting to know Derek a little better each time we came to Florida from Georgia. We attended Derek's graduation at Hurlburt. Derek was the class leader and had a large speaking part at his graduation ceremony. It was at this event that I got to witness Derek's potential as a future leader in the AF. I saw that Derek had the talent and attributes of a good public speaker (humorous, sincere, to the point).

> One afternoon Jane and I had just driven in from Georgia and went to our house in Florida where Wendy lived. I was out on the back porch drinking a beer and Jane was making dinner. Derek unexpectedly came by while Wendy was still at the Gulfarium where she worked as a dolphin trainer. She wouldn't be home for an hour. Derek drank a beer with me on the porch and I asked him some questions as to what his plans were now that he was assigned to Hurlburt. Derek started talking about Wendy and before I knew it, he asked me for my blessing to marry her. After some fatherly talk about responsibility, etc., Jane came out

> on the porch. I got Jane up to speed on our discussion and we were both excited with joy. After talking for a short time longer, Derek said he needed to leave before Wendy got home. He was going to surprise her with a proposal later that night. As he was preparing to leave, he nervously said to me, "But Col. Wild you never answered my question!" I happily gave consent and Jane hugged Derek and welcomed him into our family. Mike Wild, July 2005

While this was going on in Florida, I was on my first motorcycle trip. Opa and I had planned a trip to Alaska. One evening he came home and announced that Alaska would always be there, but that the Harley Davidson 100$^{th}$ anniversary would not. Marriage is all about compromise, so I agreed to the trip only if I rode my own bike. The problem was, I didn't know how to ride. I took the motorcycle safety class and passed the riding portion on a very small bike provided by the class. In the meantime, Opa purchased a Harley Road King for me. After only a few practice rides, I followed him to Wisconson and back. On our way home, we hit some very bad storms. One particular evening we saw the sky turn black and the weather became very dangerous. Luckily, we found a KOA camp just a few miles up. They had one cabin left and we settled in just in time.

Derek made it a habit to call me regularly on this trip to check on me. I remember the phone cutting in and out that night, but Derek was able to tell me he was going to propose to Wendy that night, buy the house from Mike and Jane, and had the surprise all planned out. He had the ring and was going to hide it from her. I remember telling him that after all of the planning, please let us know if she said Yes. He called back later that evening and I asked what her answer was. "Hell, Yes!" he said with so much excitement in his voice he could hardly contain it. He called us again the next morning to check if the weather had cleared. I told him it had and that I would not likely take another motorcycle trip unless it was for something very special. Little did I know at that time that five years later, I would make the trip again for a much different purpose. I would ride again to raise money for the Special Operations Warrior Foundation. We didn't know anything about them at the time, only that Derek had helped raise money for them on occasions. One such time was when he was a young Lt. just starting at the 23$^{rd}$. He shaved his head, but the guys left two pigtails. Of course when he walked down the hall in his uniform, he was called on the carpet for being "out of uniform." We found it funny at the time. Later, the Special Ops Warrior Foundation would play a pivotal role in our lives, and welcome us as family.

We were excited about Derek and Wendy setting the date for their wedding. One evening Derek called and said they would like to have the ceremony here at home in Lompoc. He wanted to include family and friends that could not afford to, or otherwise make it to Florida. He asked if I would mind if Wendy's brother Mike (a minister) could perform the vows early on the beach in Destin. He explained that it would just be Wendy, Mike, Libby (Mike's wife) and himself. He explained that if he should be deployed before the ceremony in Lompoc, and something happened to him, that Wendy would be taken care of. It was very important to him. On September 25, 2003 they were married on the beach in the private ceremony. The big ceremony was here in Lompoc on April 17, 2004. Derek was very excited that we understood and looked forward to the wedding here. He wanted to include all of his family and friends. I think Wendy made two trips out with friends to plan the ceremony and find a location. In the meantime, Derek continued his work and enjoyed the fishing and life on the Emerald Coast.

Every moment that he could find, your Dad would go fishing. He loved that your grandfather (Mike) had a boat and that they lived on the bayou. It made him so happy to be stationed at Hurlburt and so near the water.

*1st time out:*

*I had just gotten my new boat (24 ft Robalo Walk Around) and Derek couldn't wait to go out fishing. Derek had become an avid fisherman and had been out plenty of times in the gulf with a squadron mate who had a boat. With all of Derek's TDYs and busy schedule, it was hard to find time to get out. Derek finally took a couple days of leave and we finally found a day where the weather was marginal but ok. The sea state was 2-4 ft which can sometimes be a little rough. We went out early and caught a few keepers. We only went out about 5 miles because the seas were building. As the afternoon approached, the thunderstorms were also building and starting to surround the Destin pass. The pass can be treacherous when the storms hit. I mentioned that we should be heading in pretty soon because of the building t-storms. Derek couldn't believe that I wanted to go in! We still had another 4 to 5 hours of fishing time in the day. I had seen deteriorating weather patterns like this many times before, and the time was approaching for us to go in before the t-storms hit. Derek was obviously disappointed but we went in anyhow. As we approached the 'C' buoy which is about ¼ mile outside the pass, we saw what looked like a coast guard boat or some kind of military boat on its way out. I commented that those guys were nuts to go out in this weather . . . Derek answered, "Hey, those are guys in my squadron going out for some training . . . we do this all the time!"*

*The checkride:*

*Derek and I finally had the opportunity to go out fishing in the boat, several times in fact. We always caught some keeper-sized fish and always had a great time. I told Derek that when I thought he was comfortable with handling the boat and the electronics, he could take the boat out anytime without me. I flew for Delta Airlines and was gone a lot so there would be plenty of opportunities for Derek to take the boat out when I was gone.*

*After several outings in the boat, we went out once again and I told Derek this would be his check ride. If everything went ok, the boat would be his when Jane and I were not using it. Derek did a great job that day. He was a quick learner and mastered all the techniques to go out and catch fish. At the end of each fishing trip, I would always stop at Crab Island to relax and wash off the first layer of fish and bait grime. Crab Island is a shallow water area just inside the Destin bridge where boats assemble to anchor and swim or party. To enter or exit Crab Island, you have to carefully watch the water depth, as it varies from 6ft to 2ft very quickly. When you leave Crab Island and head in to Choctaw bay, you have to travel through a deep water channel that has very shallow water on either side. The channel makes a big circle to the west as you exit, but the channel markers are far apart, making it sometimes hard to see just where the channel is. When you finally get in to the channel and past the no wake zone, you can push it up to full speed and, as long as you stay inside the markers, there's no problem of hitting shallow water.*

*Our destination was Ben's Lake Marina on Eglin AFB which was about 3 miles across the bay. The visibility was good that day. We could see the marina area across the bay and this is where Derek steered the boat toward. As soon as we got out of the 'no wake' zone in the channel, Derek pushed it up and we were cruising home. Derek was feeling pretty cocky because he knew that he had performed well on the boat, as usual, and in a few minutes his 'check ride' would be over. Derek visually lined up with the buildings closest to the marina and headed straight toward them. What he didn't notice was the actual channel swinging to the west—the next channel markers being quite a distance away. We were now exiting the channel to the side. I looked at the depth finder and saw the water depth getting shallower and shallower. Derek was still going fast with a big grin on his face. I asked him if he knew where he was and he replied "SURE!" with that cocky attitude. I then asked how deep the water was—I saw the shallow water coming.*

*He looked at the depth finder and immediately pulled the throttle to idle and we narrowly avoided running into 1-2 ft deep water. I then mentioned that the channel markers were way to the left, and he embarrassingly said "Busted!" He knew he didn't pass the check ride and he felt terrible. Then I said jokingly "Hey, I've never done that!" Derek felt humiliated. I then told him to take us on in to the marina. Derek swallowed his pride, got us to the marina, and parked the boat perfectly. He was surprised when I shook his hand and said "You passed!" and congratulated him.*

*Derek took Wendy and Logan out several times after that. I knew that Derek could now add "proud new boat owner" to the list of all his specialties and I would never have to worry about my boat running aground with Derek behind the wheel.*

*Mike Wild, July 2005*

Jane shared some of her memories shortly after in the following letter:

*I miss Derek like he was my own son. I loved him as such. He was such a loving person . . . I wish with all my heart that I had more time with him. I laughed with him . . . his sense of humor was contagious and very surprising! He caught me off guard more than once . . . And the love he shared with everyone he cared about was so amazing . . .*

*He was a beginning (boat) fisherman and had the best luck I ever saw! I never really got to fish with him myself, but I heard about his exploits from him and from others. He had uncanny good luck . . . beginner's luck? He told me about catching a big red snapper while fishing with his buddies and using it for BAIT to catch huge grouper!! I personally would kill to catch a large red snapper to keep, and I would NOT use it as bait . . . ha! He was luckier that I could ever be. He caught fish, huge fish, and would throw them back because he didn't know what they were . . . didn't know that I would die to catch even one of them. I often teased him about his not wanting to be a bottom fisher like Mike and me. He preferred to throw out lures in a top water application to catch sport fish. Mike and I like to bottom fish with live or dead bait and catch whatever is down there. Derek told me that if he wanted to catch the fish on the bottom, he would dive down and catch them there with a spear gun! Amazing.*

*I remember when he fished off our back yard in the bayou. He would head out there every time they came to visit us and was lured by the water. He would invariably catch something, even if it was the size of his bait! He was showing off for Wendy on Thanksgiving Day of 2004. After dinner, he and Wendy and Mike went out back to fish. Derek was showing Wendy how to cast out a line. This went on for an hour or so, up and down the bank. I think Wendy got the idea in a few minutes but loved watching Derek show her. Anyhow, he left her with one pole and walked to another area and tossed out his line only to promptly fall in the water, up to his calf in slimy cold water while wearing his good shoes! He laughed about it and she did too.*

*I also remember him showing her how to use the kayaks off our back yard. He let her use his kayak and he tried to use hers. He was much larger and heavier than she was and her kayak was supposed to be for someone her size. She was paddling around out in the water in his kayak waiting for him, and he was stuck on the bank in hers, one long leg and big foot out each side of the kayak, pushing for all he was worth to get waterborne. Wendy was amused and I laughed myself silly. Jane Wild, July 2005*

Everyone would describe Derek as a Patriot. He loved the flag and all it stood for and he loved the 4$^{th}$ of July. On July 4$^{th}$ of 2005, he was due home. His team returned that night to Hurlburt without three members. I had several calls from Wendy that day, and she had made a very brave decision. I wished throughout the day that I wasn't so far away and that I could have been with her. The decision was to go and meet the plane and the other team members with you, Logan. I can't imagine how very difficult this was for her, knowing that Derek would not be stepping off. She would be there with other wives that were welcoming home their husbands and children welcoming home their dads. She knew that the team was suffering too, and this was the right thing to do. Your dad would have done the same thing and I'm sure she knew that. I always respected and loved her, but my respect and admiration for her strength grew that night. I don't recall hearing the fireworks at home that night or seeing them. Now I can watch them again and recall happier times.

From a very early age, Derek learned flag etiquette in the scouts and learned the family history of the men who fought in our family and the symbolism of the flag. He respected and honored it always and understood that it represented our freedom. Since the Civil War, the majority of the men in our family served their country. They were an example and inspiration to him.

My mother, (Momo) was the oldest of nine children. Her father and grandfather served. Of the nine children in my mother's family, all five men joined the military. She became a Navy nurse. In the history of our family, not one man was drafted. They all volunteered. This is something we are very proud of. My father (Dado) attended a private military high school and prep school in Charlotte Hall Maryland. He entered the Marine Corps at the age of 17 and was in for 21 years. On his first tour as a seagoing Marine, he was assigned to the Vincennes in the Savo Islands in the Pacific. The ship was sunk and he floated, severely wounded in the water for eight hours before he was rescued. When he was able, he returned to battle again. Towards the end of the war in 1944, he was shot through the chest on Iwo Jima. It was during his recovery period at the Naval hospital in Portsmouth Virginia, that he met my mother.

In 1863, your great-uncle four times removed, Elisha Stockwell wrote home to his mother about the 4th of July and the flag, while he was serving in the Civil War.

> "Respected mother,
>
> *I received a letter from you some time ago and have answered it, but I thought I would write a few lines to you to let you know that I got into Vicksburg at last alive and well. We came in on the day of the 4th of July. We had a happy fourth you may bet. We came in with Logan's division. The stars and stripes were hoisted on the court house and we marched down on main street in front of the court house and gave three cheers for the flag of our union. We stayed in town until night and then went back to our old camping ground. It was the happiest fourth I ever spent."*
>
> *Private Elisha Stockwell, Jr. Company I,*
> *Fourteenth Wisconsin Volunteer Regiment*
> *(From the book, "Private Elisha Stockwell, Jr. Sees the Civil War")*

Derek wrote his own letter about the flag and what it meant to him in the 6th grade in December of 1988.

### WHY WE SHOULD HONOR OUR FLAG

**The flag of our country is a symbol. It is a symbol of our Freedom, Justice and Honor. The flag is honored in many ways in our country. One way is when we say**

the Pledge of Allegiance. Do we really understand the words we are saying?

"I pledge allegiance to the flag, of the United States of America."

To me, this line means you are swearing your loyalty to the symbol that represents the United States.

"And to the Republic for which it stands"

A Republic is a government in which the supreme power is with the citizens, and their right to vote.

"One Nation, Under God"

Even though we are represented separately on the flag, one star for each state, we all come together in the blue background as one group, all together in the eyes of God.

"Indivisable with liberty and justice for all"

To me this means we are a nation that will never be divided again like we were in the civil war. Also, we are a nation that welcomes everybody.

This pledge is the best way we can show how much we love and honor our country. Another way we can honor the flag is at Memorial Day. On this day we should put the flag out at our homes, and go to the service at the cemetery. On this day we show respect to the veterans of the wars who risked their lives or were killed protecting our freedom and our flag. I am happy to see them put a little flag on my Grandfather's grave.

**If I could change one thing to show more respect to the flag, I would say not to burn it if it touches the ground. We should pick it up, shake it out and hang it up again.**

**By Derek Mears Argel**

**6th Grade, Ms. Schade, Vandenberg Middle School**

Derek never had a problem as a child or an adult reminding people to remove their hats for the pledge or to let them know in a kind way about respect for the flag.

One July 4th while your Dad was attending the Academy, he was able to be home at the same time as Johnny. Opa and I had been helping with the local fireworks show for the past couple of years. During set up, they came to the stadium a little early to help with setting up. Almost in unison, they said, "Do you see that flag?" At a home across the street the American flag was upside down, a sign of distress. Both your Dad and uncle were over there in a flash. They approached the door of the resident and showed him the flag. The older man couldn't see well when he put it up and asked the guys to please fix it for him. They both came back with huge grins on their faces and resumed helping us set up for the show.

It was this love for country, for God and for the flag and all it represented to him that made your father happy. It is here that I will pause to say that because of this, I don't keep the folded flag on display in our home. I never have and never will. Although I have used the folded flag as a metaphor in public speaking, it is up to the families about how that is interpreted. To me, it meant that after your father's funerals and services, people went home,they went back to their lives and continued on. I personally choose to not pack a folded flag in my luggage I spoke of earlier. I choose to remember it flying and waving in the breeze just as your father loved it and protected it with his life as a true patriot. Your dad would have never settled for the folded flag as an ending to any of his brothers or their memories.

Because of his love of the flag, Independence Day and fireworks, Opa and I decided to surprise your mother and dad with an early 4th for their wedding ceremony here in Lompoc. The rehearsal dinner was to be held the night before the wedding on April 16, 2004. As I mentioned, Opa and I had been doing pyro shows for a couple of years. One of our crew members pulled up one day with a truck about one month earlier. The Sherriff's department in Santa Barbara had taken some large fireworks off of a local celebrity's ranch. Our crew member was told to dispose of the fireworks, but did not say how. We agreed to store them in our shed for a month and thought about how to dispose of them.

I decided to cook the rehearsal dinner myself, and include the friends and family that had come in that day. We had about 50 guests. Your grandfather Wild invited his friends, and it was our first meeting with most everyone on your mother's side of the family. Our house has a parking lot across the street. We had guests park their cars facing our home in the parking lot. While everyone ate, members of the Pyro crew worked to set up a great show to rival the city fireworks show. Dressed all in black, they went unnoticed while the guests ate and enjoyed themselves. Your dad had no clue about it. When I was given the notice, I told the guests out front that something wonderful was going to happen. Derek was very excited . . . when suddenly we shot off the best American show of fireworks that the city had only seen on the 4th. It was a wonderful treat for everyone and made your Dad so happy. We shot them off while playing a tape of the Star Spangled Banner in the background. Because your parent's real wedding took place on September 25th, you were already on the way. Derek was so happy and mentioned . . . well, my son is probably doing cartwheels in Wendy's stomach over these fireworks!

This letter comes from one of Wendy's friends. Tasha was there when Derek and Wendy met, and also part of the wedding party who witnessed the great fireworks show.

*Dear Logan,*

*I have several great memories of your Dad but two specific good ones come to mind. Your mom and I were best friends and having a fun night together at McGuire's in Destin, Florida. In walked your Dad, the tallest and the most handsome of the group of guys he was with. He caught your Mom's eye but he seemed a little shy. Later that night, he said "hi" to her and they ended up talking for hours. It was fun to see them meet and watch their relationship grow. Your Mom was the happiest I had seen her and was so excited to start a future with your Dad.*

*The second great memory of your Dad was when he came out to visit my husband and I in San Diego, California. He was on a business trip and we were able to spend some time with him. We were at a fun restaurant one night having a good time. Ryan and your Dad started talking about their future careers in the military and I will always remember your Dad saying, "I just want my son to be proud of me." It was very important to him and yet you were only about 6 months old.*

*I also have some great memories of your Mom and Dad's wedding, a wonderful Christmas spent with your parents and many funny conversations on the phone with your Dad. He will always be a part of my family's loving memories and we will always miss him.*

*Natasha and Ryan Anderson, April 2012*

Natasha and the woman who writes this next letter, met and became friends through Derek. Both of their husbands are in similar jobs in the military.

*Dear Logan,*

*Your father, as I'm sure everyone has shared with you, was a really unique and incredible guy. I met him in 6<sup>th</sup> grade at Vandenberg Middle School. We were great friends throughout high school at Cabrillo, and our friendship extended into the years after we had both graduated college. So many of the most vivid and best high school memories that*

*I can recall, your Dad was a part of them. There were bonfires at the beach, swim meets, movies, get togethers with friends, French class, Senior Class Ditch Day, the Disneyland trip and Graduation. Even after college, we still talked periodically as he ventured into his Air Force career. He was one of the handful of friends I kept in touch with. I have many wonderful memories of your Dad, but the two that make me smile the most are these:*

*My birthday is on Christmas Day, which, let's face it . . . is not the ideal day to be born, really. mainly because when you're a kid (and it's all about presents and YOU!) you want to have your own special day to celebrate with your friends, most families are out of town on vacation for the holidays. It's tough to have any real type of celebration. Your birthday gets completely overshadowed by the commercialization and festivities of that time of year. While in high school, a group of my closest friends would always come over Christmas evening and help celebrate with me. Your Dad was one of those friends. That group consisted of Derek, Rohini Bali, Charlotte Hufschmidt, Paul Kendrick, and Lawrence Rodriguez. It meant so much to me to have my birthday acknowledged. We'd share my traditional Baskins Robbins' ice cream cake, maybe go to a movie, or just hang out at my house and laugh. Year after year most of that group was there, including your Dad. I remember multiple times where he'd chat with my Dad about his desire to join the Air Force, as my Dad was a retired C-130 pilot who had served 22 years. They had great conversations and your Dad was full of respect in his manner and interactions with adults. My parents always thought he was so polite and courteous.*

*These gatherings extended into the years after we had all graduated from Cabrillo, with each of us in different areas. Every year during that time frame, whoever was in town would always come by Christmas evening. He was there for so many of those years. He was that type of friend: loyal, dependable, sincere and caring. He had this funny, almost quirky sense of humor, but it was completely endearing. His ramblings made you roll your eyes sometimes, but always laugh alongside with him. He was so entertaining with his random knowledge and facts about things like African Tree Frogs or some other obscure creature or species. I have no idea where he obtained all of these crazy stories and interesting factoids. You couldn't help but listen, be captivated by it, with a huge smile on your face. That mischievous ear to ear grin of his was almost a smirk. It made you wonder what he was up to or what he was thinking about at that moment. He had such a great personality. He was quiet and reserved and never boastful. I found that he opened up more around his friends. People wanted to be his friend and wanted to be around him.*

*Another memory that demonstrates the kind of person your father was, were the numerous swim meets and Cabrillo Athletic events we had in common. I was a cheerleader throughout my 4 years at Cabrillo and cheered on your Dad in countless water polo games. He was an amazing athlete, as I know many people have relayed to you. He towered above everyone else with his height, had such presence, and was so physically strong. He and your Uncle Johnny definitely left their mark on all Cabrillo Aquatics* events. It was incredible to watch both of them play water polo and swim. Derek was so graceful for his stature, he just glided swiftly through the water with astonishing speed and made it look easy, effortless. I remember one swim meet in particular where Coach Bob Lawrence had put me in an event I was not thrilled about competing in . . . the 500 Freestyle. I was a decent swimmer, but did not have the extensive years of training and experience as your Dad and Uncle Johnny. I remember dreading having to participate in it, and Derek was so encouraging, telling me it was no big deal, to pace myself, and just relax throughout it. "Keep a good, smooth pace, don't get tense or think about it too much," he had said. During that event, I could see him out of the corner of my eye for a split second every time I approached my flip turn at the wall. I didn't realize it, but he was counting for me at the end of the lane, flashing the numbers to let me know what lap I was on and cheering me on in the process. I completely admired and looked up to him from an athletic and swimming ability perspective, asking his advice about how to get my best times for my events. He made those years at swim meets each season so enjoyable and memorable. I would not have had as much fun as I did if he hadn't been a part of it.

I smile every time I think about what an incredible guy your Dad was. I am so honored that I got to be his friend.

*Ann (Laws) Freeman, April, 2012*

# Eight

It is strange what a mother thinks about and worries about. You try to protect your children from all kinds of hurt, both physically and mentally. It is easier when you are around them, trying your best to help them become a better person than you were. I think that is always in the forefront of a parents mind. We want them to learn from our mistakes, to feel our constant love and companionship wherever life leads them. You want to take their pain away, to carry it yourself and to shoulder what might come their way. This feeling never leaves a parent who loves her children. I didn't really worry when Derek was deployed. I didn't know where he went, but knew I was not supposed to ask. I remembered that he was well trained, loved his work and that wherever he went, he had those tools in his belt that he always talked about. The greatest tools in his belt were his faith and his heart. Although he was 6'6" and in very good shape, everyone that knew him said his heart was the biggest muscle in his body. I think the following note helped me to understand a little more about his work and his contribution.

> *For those not that familiar with the military, they need to know how very special Derek was to his country and to the Global War on Terror. I can tell you from personal experience that the Combat Control Teams, the highly selective group that Derek*

*excelled with, are the Tip of the Spear for the United States Air Force. This elite group of Special Operators has been the United States Air Force's most valuable asset over the past three+ years. Derek and his Brother's in Arms have produced outstanding results in the harshest most austere conditions at great personal risk and sacrifice. They have achieved victories that most folks are not aware of. They have gone willingly and done things, good things, on behalf of their country and for people of other countries. Due to the sensitive nature of Derek's profession, most people will never really know the specifics of his contributions. Please know that Derek was an outstanding Airman. As an Air Force pilot, fellow Californian, fellow USAFA Preppie, proud fraternity of Air Force Academy Water Polo players and member of the Special Operations community, I am extremely proud to call Derek family. I am awed and humbled by his performance in life.*

*"Dan" Director, C-17 Special Operations Division, June 2005*

I don't have many stories from the deployments, nor am I privy to any special missions including the one he was on that fateful Memorial Day. That remains classified. There are a few great stories that just talk about time spent with your Dad on deployments. One of these stories was shared at a reunion in casual conversation. I thought it was a great story and Ben was happy to write it down for you.

*Dear Logan,*

*My name is Ben Hannigan. I'm a Combat Controller that worked with your father at the 23rd Special Tactics Squadron and deployed with him to Afghanistan. I'm sure that you've heard many interesting and wonderful stories about your father. He was a great man and there is no shortage of great stories about him. My story will not be the funniest or the most sentimental* that you've heard, but because of the admiration and respect that I have for him, I'd like to share with you my memory of the last time that I spoke with your father in person.

As you know, during his final deployment to Afghanistan and Iraq, Derek led the landing zone control and survey team and, between missions, he worked in the Special Tactics Operations Command (STOC). I was in Afghanistan at the same time and I worked with an army team stationed at a forward firebase separate from the base that housed the STOC. Most of the contact that I had with my friends, co-workers and command at the STOC, including Derek ("Captain Argel" to me), was accomplished via radio transmission.

At one point, my team was planning a mission with another team stationed elsewhere, so we met at a central location which happened to be the base with the STOC. We were only there for a little over twelve hours and our schedule was very tight. Although I had no obligation to do so and very little time to spare, I made it a point to visit my friends at the STOC. Derek happened to be between missions that night and he was there. It was so nice to see everyone and just to be around familiar faces that my visit lasted longer than I had planned and I was running late. Rather than walk back to where I needed to meet my team Derek offered to drive me back to save time. As we were pulling out of the STOC compound, he suddenly stopped the truck, looked at me and asked, "Do you need a knife?"

It seemed to be an out of place question, but everyone needs a knife and I just happened to have broken mine about a week earlier, "uh well . . . yeah actually, I do. Why? How did you know that?"

"I just remembered that we got some fixed-blade, Bench Made, knives in a few days ago. They're really nice, I'll get one." He *put the truck in park, jumped out and ran back to the STOC. Minutes later he returned with a brand new knife and handed it to me. As he started driving again he said, "Never say I didn't give you something to remember me by."*

*Why your father chose that phrase, I'll never know. Maybe it was for lack of something better to say and designed to avoid an uncomfortable silence like so many things that people say . . . . Maybe it was a subconscious choice of words. The knife is a piece of military issued equipment that Derek didn't pay for or acquire himself and doesn't exactly qualify as a gift; especially not a gift to help you "remember" someone. At this time, I just chuckled and said "O.K. Sir. Thanks. I'll use this. I just broke my other knife a little while ago."*

*We pulled up to the compound where I needed to go. We got out and did our "man hugs" where you shake hands, bump your chests together (with arms in between of course) and slap each other on the back. "Alright. Stay safe . . ." Derek told me. "Will do, Sir. You too."*

*"O.K . . . , see ya," he said and drove off as I walked into the compound. Though I had some e-mail type conversations with him over the radio in the following weeks, I never did see him again. However, the words that Derek uttered when he gave me the knife rung in my head when I heard about his death. The knife went from a "military issued piece of equipment" to a gift that helps me remember a great man, just like he said. I still use the knife even though I now think of it as a momento. It's meant to be used and I'll use it for as long as it works. Every time I use it, I think of Captain Derek Argel. I'll "never say that he didn't give me something to remember him by."*

*With heartfelt respect and gratitude for the sacrifice that you had to endure without choice and the sacrifice that your father so generously and honorably chose to offer,* Ben Hannigan, November 2006

The night Ben shared this with me, I was so thankful. It just sounded so much like Derek. He liked to collect knives and cherished his first boy scout knife and Swiss Army knife. One Christmas, he wanted a very special knife that was just on the market. It was a Titanium 2000, rust resistant and all for diving. He loved to give knives as gifts to those he thought of. I'm certain that he gave this knife to Ben on that evening because he thought so much of him. I'm sure it was his own military issue. I asked Ben where the knife was that night. He said he always carried it with him. Of course I asked if I could see it and hold it. As the picture was being taken of me with the knife I accidently cut myself with it, but we got the picture!

Just before Christmas in 2004, Derek ordered about 150 knives to give out as gifts. Wendy said that with this order he got (in her words) a very scary looking big one. He thought it was a showpiece and should hang in their bedroom. I think Wendy won that round and the knife was not displayed there.

During deployments everyone appreciated mail time and receiving packages. We tried to make sure that there was always a package or two on the way to Derek. He always had specific requests for himself and the other guys he would be sharing with. Every tiny space in the flat rate boxes from the post office would be filled. I got the large commercial bags of beef jerky from Bruce, our local butcher in Lompoc. Derek also requested red vines, gum, men's health magazines and hard candy. A few times I found some inexpensive DVD movies that were not best sellers. I was reminded of this recently when I read through some of Derek's emails. On February 26, 2005 he wrote:

"Hey Ma,

**How are things back home? It was good to see that Uncle Jack and Aunt Sue stopped by to see Wendy and the little man when they were out there. That would also be nice if they moved out to Florida, that way when you guys get out there momo will be able to visit them. How is John doing? Anything new to report on his end? Well I'm about to go get some chow, but just wanted to drop a line to say hi. Remember when you guys come out next, I'm going to have a boat, so tell Todd to be prepared. As far as the packages, it doesn't matter what you put in there, just so long as it's not any more budget movies. Those only make for good objects to throw at other people. Give my love to everyone and let them know all is well. Love, Me"**

Wendy and I sent packages at about the same time so they would be there for his birthday on March 11. My mother added a few things to my box with a card. Always cheering us up with a little humor, on March 17 of 2005 he wrote:

"Hey Ma,

**Thanks for the box of goodies on the b-day mom. I really do appreciate the goodies from both you and Todd. Well things here are starting to get a little busy and that's a good thing because it makes the time go by faster. Tell John I wish he was with me here as well. He said that in his letter. I miss the hell out of him too. Tell momo thank you for her card and the 5 cents for the soda. I don't know when the last time momo drank a soda was, but inflation sucks. Well ma, I really look forward to seeing both you and Todd in the near future. We'll all have our hands full with little man. He should be around**

**one when you guys come out so he should be fun. I love you guys and will talk to you soon. Love, me"**

The next letter comes from Carrie, who got to know Derek during his first deployment. This one touches both on Derek's serious and comical side.

*Dear Logan,*

*I don't know where to begin to talk about your Dad, the larger than life Derek Argel. I do take comfort in knowing that your Dad, Jeremy and Casey are all in heaven and by God's grace I will see all three of them again there someday. I really didn't know Derek very well until I was deployed with him in 2004 during his first deployment. Now this deployment in 2005 is coming to an end and I know that I need to write you this letter to tell you some of my memories of your Dad. I'm sure you'll hear a lot of great stories about your Dad, and hopefully I can share a few with you that you haven't heard.*

*The first memory that comes into my head is last year in Afghanistan on his first deployment and during our first rocket attack at the base. It was nighttime and two rockets impacted the north side of the base, we were located further to the south. Finally, the alarm sounded telling everyone to take cover. Your dad came out of the Operations Center, dressed in all his kit which included his body armor, his M-4 rifle, all his magazines fully loaded, his helmet, his night vision goggles and he was shouting for the rest of the operators to get their kit on and meet him on top of the bunker. He told the rest of us to get in the bunker for cover. Your dad stayed on top of the bunker ready to fight the bad guys. I still to this day have no idea who he thought he was going to fight, but he was sure ready. He stayed up there waiting to kill the enemy, until the all clear was sounded. It was too funny because, usually the rocket attacks are just harassing fire and on timers, so there's no enemy even close by, but he was ready! Everyone in our unit has operating initials, what we're called. Your dad was known to most of us as AL. After that incident on top of the bunker, we started calling him TF AL, meaning Task Force Argel, because he was a one man task force.*

*Another one from that deployment in 2004, is just an example of how competitive he was. He heard that one of his buddies could eat the two crackers from an MRE without drinking anything, then whistle afterward. Well, he tried it once, but didn't have a witness, so the next day he asked me to time him and be his witness. Well, I timed him and sure enough he ate the crackers and was able to whistle in less than two minutes, even though it was a struggle. I even got a picture of him trying to eat those crackers. He also would ride the mini bike once in a while during that deployment just to take it out for a spin around the flightline which was always an interesting sight; your Dad's 6'6 frame on a tiny motorcycle, I'm not sure how he even rode that thing.*

*Towards the end of 2004, your Dad, Jeremy, Mason, Jason and I all participated in an event called a Monster Mash at Hurlburt Field. It's a type of race with a lot of different events, anything from running, to swimming, to shooting, to an obstacle course and to different stations to include setting up a radio and putting a weapon together with a bag over your head. Well, these guys decided they wanted to win with an all officer team. That's where they ran into a problem, they couldn't find another officer, so they asked me. Granted, I'm an officer, but I'm a girl who probably wasn't going to lead these hard core guys to victory, if anything they'd be dragging me along. I was especially concerned about your Dad, because I knew he was competitive and I didn't want to let him down or get yelled at. Well, the race turned out to be tiring and exhausting, but a lot of fun. I think we ran 9 miles that day. Your dad was well in front of the rest of the team, when he came to the final station, which was putting together an M-4 with a bag on your head. Now, the team was supposed to talk the person who was covered through this as a team event, we just couldn't touch the weapon. When the rest of the team ran up to the station, your Dad was there, with the bag on his head already putting the weapon back together. I was impressed, we were able to help him a little, but he put a lot of it together before we even got there. We didn't come in first that day . . . we were second; we were robbed of the victory because the winning team cheated, but that's another story.*

*This year, 2005, found your Dad and I on the same deployment again. Of course this was a year later and he was more experienced this time around. He was really fortunate on this deployment because he was able to operate and go out on more missions. It was a great opportunity for him, because usually officers didn't get to go out on missions. He was able to go on protection details, providing security for the US Ambassador to Afghanistan. He usually went on Operating initials, AL, but while on this mission he started going by Al. Instead of saying A and L, he said his name was Al. People started calling our Ops center asking for Al, and at first we didn't know who they were asking for, because none of us called him Al. Basically he was protecting his identity, but it was funny to hear him called by another name.*

*I remember one day, he got an email from your Mom and he told me that you had started swimming lessons. I said, but Logan's not even a year old. He said proudly, "that's my boy" I think you were only ten months old at the time. I also enjoyed giving your Dad a hard time, because it was fun. I said, what if Logan doesn't like swimming. Your dad said you would and you'd play water polo. I came back and said, what if he wants to play football, AL said, water polo, I said track, he said water polo. I think I was starting to irritate him, but it was all in fun.*

*I know he was so proud of you. He kept a picture of you as the wallpaper on his computer.*

*Your dad was serious about his job and loved what he did and loved the guys he worked with. He also appreciated everyone who helped support him to accomplish the mission. For him, the job was so important. Writing this letter doesn't do your Dad justice. He was passionate about everything and certainly shared his opinion. I just wanted you to know some of my memories of your Dad. I didn't really know your Mom, but I have met her, I can tell you that I know she is a very strong lady. On the day of the crash, she wrote a letter to all the men he worked with. The letter was posted in our operations center right next to where I worked and every time one of the guys read the letter, they got choked up and said basically the same thing, they said Wendy is an amazing woman, and so strong.*

*Logan, I may never meet you when you're older, but please know that I pray for you and your Mom. It was truly an honor knowing your Dad, Derek, even though it was for such a short amount of time. Carrie Brant (June 2006)*

There were so many stories about his time deployed. Some were just verbally shared with me. I think it was on Memorial Day of 2006 at the cemetery in Lompoc, that Todd and I walked back to Derek's memorial there. When we walked up, two medics introduced themselves to us. The woman said she met Derek at Baghram Air Base. She went to the gym to work out and wanted to do squats. Derek had just left that station and forgot to take the weight off. She was a small woman and introduced herself and asked that he take the heavy weight off he had just been lifting. He apologized and removed the weight. She told him that some of the medics were having a BBQ that evening and would he and some of the other CCT guys like to join them. He said "sure." She related to me that she collected money from the others and purchased Brats to be brought back from Germany . . . and was very proud of this. When the CCT guys came for the BBQ, they brought steaks . . . and she wondered how they got them. She said one day that she spotted Derek speaking to a higher ranking officer and pulled a cold steak out of his pocket to eat during their conversation. With Derek's eating habits, I told her this didn't surprise me.

This last year, Todd and I went to the mini-reunion in Las Vegas for CCT. As I said, this is normally an event for retired CCT but in 2011, we had some active guys that were there for training. We were happy that they could join us for a short time one evening. We had been at your Uncle K's the evening before for a BBQ, and told him and the other pilots (Dustin too) about the mini-reunion. They told us there were guys there for training and we invited them to join us the next evening . . . if they got the word out.

Something had been bothering me for some time. In the case that was dedicated to Derek at the Academy, there was mention of an Operation. He was listed as the sole air support for this Marine operation providing close air support, air assault, re-supply and medical evacs. At the BBQ, I told Derek's friends that I would like any information about this. They said they had none. This mission was listed in 2005 and referred to as "harsh terrain." The next evening, sitting at my table, a man approached me with one of the funniest stories I had heard. It so happened it was a story about the mission that I had been thinking about. I've changed the wording just a little but it reads like something right out of a MASH episode. It shows Derek's humor, his humanitarian side, but most of all that guys deployed together make the best out of what they have.

> *I was a Tactical Air Control Party (TACP) member at the time and I was assigned to do a joint operation with Marines in Afghanistan in 2005. Capt Argel and I were paired together and*

we were tasked to work a long mission together. On the first night of the mission, he and I were sitting on the tail of a Humvee when Derek said, "CL, I think that Army guy is going through your bag." I look back and saw what was going on and we went over to confront the guy and he said he needed pants. When Derek asked "why?" he said, "because mine are messed up." Derek asked where his other pants were and he said those were also messed up. At this point I lost it and couldn't control my laughter and Derek tried to keep a straight face but kept snickering. Then Derek asked if he had a sleeping bag he could get into and he said he had also 'messed up' his sleeping bag and boots. At this point we were laughing so hard I was almost crying. So Derek and I had to go up to every Marine that was out there with us and ask if they had any extra pants. Most Marines asked "why?" and Derek and I could barely contain our laughter and just respond, "because we need them." We ended up finding a Marine that happened to have sweatpants in his ruck, but no one had any extra boots. In the meantime, Derek called in a MEDEVAC for the Army guy because he determined he was unfit to continue on the operation. When we called it into the Marine Command he read them the standard MEDEVAC request, but they sternly questioned why he wanted to have him MEDEVAC'd out. Derek frankly said, "He has messed up both pairs of pants, his boots and his sleeping bag . . . he is a liability." After a long and awkward pause on the radio they came back and said they'd send the helicopter, but you could tell now they were trying to keep their composure and keep from laughing on the radio. So now a helicopter was on the way and all we had for the Army guy was Marine sweat pants. So Derek and the Medic knew he'd need shoes, so they ripped apart some Meals-Ready-to-Eat (MRE) boxes and wrapped them around the guys feet and tied them off with 550 parachute cord. We also managed to find a rain jacket for the guy also. The funniest part of the night was watching the guy (who was a dead ringer for the character "Milky" from the *movie Me, Myself, and Irene) walk out to the helicopter with his sweatpants, cardboard shoes and rain jacket. Once on the helicopter it was not over, the helicopters didn't listen to Derek's direction and flew right over where the Marines had set up small personal tents and blew some of them over while they were still in them. It was honestly one of the funniest things I have ever seen in the military. CL (February 2012)*

Derek was a humanitarian, I'm sure was determined to help this guy out no matter what. I'm sure it also provided a little comic relief during a serious mission.

Logan, as I mentioned in the beginning, I never really worried when your Dad was deployed as I never knew where he was. It would be something like a "vacation" call. Through these stories, we have a glimpse of a few of the things he did and some of the kinds of missions he was on.

One of the things he did was provide security and support for high ranking officials and very special visitors in the zone.

I'm jumping ahead now to May 2010. Most of the time over the past few years, I have had some fundraiser to attend or I have tried to stay busy on Memorial Day. After the service at the Lompoc cemetery, I got a call from my mother. Her neighbor asked if we had read the new book, "Spoken from the Heart" by Laura Bush. She said that Derek was mentioned on page 313. We rushed over to the book store and picked up a copy. Of course I went right to that page. I wrote Mrs. Bush and thanked her for including Derek. In my letter, I explained that because of her recounting of the time spent in Afghanistan with Derek, we almost got to take a virtual mission with my son. Through her eyes, we felt like we were on the helicopter and looking down at the terrain in Afghanistan. It was a remarkable gift to us. She wrote back promptly sending her best to our family. I keep her note card in back of your dad's picture on the fireplace. Derek of course never said anything about it. When I met President Bush at the White House a couple of years earlier, I told him that Derek described Mrs. Bush to someone as the most gracious lady he ever met. Because he could not use her name, he told a CCT brother he escorted "The main man's squeeze." I have a great picture of Opa and President Bush with their arms around each other's shoulders at the White house. We were all laughing when I related the story.

Another picture I have on my wall is of Derek with the U.S. Ambassador to Afghanistan in 2005, Zalmay Khalilzad. He wrote to General Eikenberry shortly after that picture was taken.

*Dear General Eikenberry,*

*I would like to extend my thanks and appreciation to LT Derek Argel of the 23rd Special Tactics Squadron for his outstanding professionalism and support during my recent trip on May 4, 2005 to Kandahar. LT Argel provided the vital ground to air communications interface for my protection detail and the U.S. Army rotary wing assets. He controlled the attack helicopters and coordinated the landing of the transport helicopters thus facilitation the efficient and effective arrival of my official entourage during this very important visit. His expertise and skill in managing the air operations enabled my Security Protection Detail to focus on motorcade operations and the personal ring security for myself including protection for the British Ambassador and the Deputy Minister of Information and Culture.*

*Once again thank you for a job well done. It is this spirit of cooperation that will sustain our mission here in Afghanistan.*

*The professionalism of LT Argel exemplifies the True American Spirt.*

*Sincerely,
Zalmay Khalilzad, Ph.D, Ambassador and Special Presidential Envoy*

In June of 2005 he wrote:

*Derek was assigned as combat controller to provide overhead support for me in addition to his regular duties. His professionalism greatly impressed all of us, and the Ambassador's Security Detail requested that he serve as combat controller for all my subsequent movements. Derek was very thorough, extremely precise, and a meticulous planner—just the qualities needed in someone responsible for a critical security operation. His job also included the coordination of many assets and personnel in a high-pressure situation. Everything about his manner provided an air of reassurance, and it was obvious that he felt a strong dedication to excellence. Derek was called upon to serve in this capacity whenever I moved outside of Kabul, which meant that we had an opportunity to get to know him personally.*

*You should take solace in knowing that Derek passionately believed in doing his duty, and that he felt honored to have had the opportunity to serve his country. We, in turn, felt honored to have served with him.*

# Nine

One of the greatest influences in your dad's life was my Uncle Jack. In my lifetime, I have called on him many times. He provided strength and guidance for Derek and his goals for the military. Derek loved him and his Aunt Sue, and so appreciated both them and his cousins for being part of his life.

> Dear Logan,
>
> As I sit here today writing this letter to you, I realize that you will probably not be reading it for some years. The purpose of the letter is to give you some idea and understanding of who your biological father was and what he meant to friends and family from different perspectives. Understandably, you were too young to likely have any personal recollection of him. He was so proud of you, as we all were of him. Logan, please remember that none of this is meant to detract in any way whatsoever from your second, wonderful adoptive father who has cared for you and raised you as his own. We all owe him a huge debt of gratitude for his love for you and your mother.
>
> Your father was a giant of a man in so many respects, whose compassion, consideration and soul matched his brute size. He

*was fondly referred to by friends and family alike as the gentle giant. At the time of his death, he was doing exactly what he had always dreamed of and aspired to do: proudly serving his God and Country in the best and most effective way possible in whatever capacity required of him. As a Captain in Special Operations in the US Air Force, his position was perfectly suited to that mission. He was looked upon as a genuine hero by his extended family.*

*Derek demonstrated his compassion and affinity for the underdog in a number of unselfish and admirable ways. I was always struck by his devotion and kindness toward his maternal grandmother, who was a nurturing influence in his formative years. On another, important day in his life, he took the time and displayed his bent for looking out for the less fortunate. At the Air Force Academy Graduation in 2001 the whole family was in attendance, and our son and his family had gone with us from Phoenix, AZ. He brought his step-daughter with him. She was nine years old at that time and she was your father's second cousin. There is a long standing tradition at the service academies that after each graduation ceremony is completed, the cadets toss their hats into the air in one big group. All the young kids in the bleachers are allowed to storm onto the field and try and get a hat for a treasured souvenir. Derek's cousin was a little shy at that age, and she was out-hustled and failed to snag a hat for herself. She was mighty disappointed, but Derek consoled by saying that he would see about procuring a hat for her. Typical of his thoughtfulness, at breakfast the next morning, he presented her with a hat, not of the throwaway kind, but one of his dress uniform hats with a generous monetary gift stuffed in the hatband. She was thrilled and to this day that hat hangs in a place of honor in her bedroom. Such was his enduring habit of thinking of others.*

*Logan, you are a lucky fellow in several respects. First you had a father who brought you into this world . . . a super dad who loved you and your Mom dearly. When he was gone, one of his friends kept in touch with you and Mom, fell in love with her and married her vowing to love, protect and cherish you both with all his heart. He has shown you the unique love that is only possible between a father and son and has loved you as his own. And then beautiful Evie and Luke made the scene, to love and enjoy as a little sister and brother. Wow! How very special is that?*

*You have had two strong father figures in your life, one to be remembered if only through the eyes of others, and one to love, honor and respect as he has guided you in life in good times and bad, standing beside you, guiding and advising you as only a father can.*

*By the time you read this, you will be well along the road into your future. May you grow and prosper in God's light, and may His richest blessing follow you faithfully through life. As we say in the Navy, "May you always have fair winds and following seas." Our hopes and prayers go with you always.*

*Your loving great, great uncle and aunt,
Jack and Sue Henderson (May 2011)*

Early on the morning of graduation from the Academy, each squadron had a separate ceremony to pin the rank of $2^{nd}$ Lt., making the cadets officially officers. Derek told me earlier that we would not be able to hug each other during the ceremony. He said that would be a public display of affection in his uniform. Because of his last name, he was called up first for the pinning on of his rank. Johnny and I each pinned the rank on each shoulder board. We were so proud, but didn't hug him. Needless to say, each officer that came up after Derek hugged his or her family members. After this happened repeatedly, I turned around to where Derek was seated. He gave me a "sorry" gesture as if to say, "I didn't know." After each officer was pinned and the applause was over, I saw Derek go forward and pick up the microphone. He asked the audience for their attention and promptly said, "I didn't get to hug my family, so I would like them to come forward now for a hug." Everyone went wild with applause, and again I was very proud.

*Dear Logan,*

*My letter to you starts with how I met your (grandmother) Oma. I was a bit of a wild man back then and I think she was somewhat scared at first due to the leather jacket and long hair. Meeting Oma for the first time I knew she was a very special woman and within one year I would ask her to marry me. Your Dad was the first person I contacted after she said yes and asked him if 3/23 would be a date he could possibly get leave for.*

*I had no idea he was assigned to the 23rd Special Tactics Squadron at that point so the date was even more special upon finding that out.*

*Prior to meeting Oma I had planned on riding my Harley back to Laconia, New Hampshire, for Bike week. My life and priorities took a big change when I met Oma and what was to become my new family. Derek was to graduate from the Air Force Academy around that same time and due to all of Derek's struggles and hard work to reach that goal he had set for himself I opted to cancel my road trip to attend his graduation in Colorado Springs.*

*Vice President Cheney personally handed out all the diplomas and it was a very moving experience to see and hear first hand what Derek had accomplished, we were all so very proud of him.*

*I was never in the military, however I did try to enlist in the Marine Corp upon graduating from high school and was rejected due to being asthmatic and was told I was exempt from all branches of the Armed Forces due to my disease. Respect for the military and all of the sacrifices made by so many has always been very important to me and felt it was my civic duty to join. Needless to say I walked away rejected and disappointed.*

*With your father "no and rejection" was not acceptable and he would always strive to correct an issue to allow himself to move forward. It was one of the very many qualities that made him the man he was.*

*After graduation we all drove back home in a caravan stopping over in Las Vegas due to the late hour. As your Dad had been assigned to Hurlburt Air Force Base and would only be home briefly, he was anxious to continue home driving thru the night and I was game to do so as well. We decided to leave it up to Momo. Your Dad asked her; "Well Momo, should we BULL DAWG thru the night?" Her response was sincere and funny the way she said it, "LETS BULL DAWG."*

*After getting married Oma and Opa decided to ride Harleys back to Wisconsin for the 100$^{th}$ anniversary of Harley Davidson. Everyone was trying to talk Oma out of riding her own bike due to not having any experience. When we discussed the matter with your Dad he encouraged Oma to do so and backed us up with the fact that anyone can do anything if they put their hearts and minds into it. He was thinking of buying a bike himself, and on a quick visit home took Oma's 1996 Road King out for a spin. He dwarfed the bike and asked if they made anything bigger due* to his size. We all just laughed because it reminded me of the Kiwani's club riding mini bikes in a parade.

While we were on our trip, Oma received a call from Derek stating he had just met the woman of his dreams, your mother. We would continue to get calls as he was trying to win her heart over. Due to the fact that Oma used to work with dolphins and he found out that your Mom was doing that, he needed some common ammo to better deliver his conversation to her. He was so funny and we were so happy to hear he had met that special person. It was not long after that that Derek called to tell us he was going to ask for her hand in marriage. Soon after they were married and we were to be blessed with the news that you Logan, were on the way.

We wanted to be there when you were born and help in any way we could. We landed in Florida and got to the hospital just a half hour before you arrived. Your dads smile was as big as the Whopper he had in his hand after we were brought in to see you for the first time. One hand was on you and one on the Whopper.

Fishing was another love of your dads and we would be off in Grampa Mike's boat fishing in the Gulf the very next morning after you were born. We reeled in the lunkers and had a great time together.

After your dad's passing in Iraq, Oma and Opa set our goals to support the Special Operations Warrior Foundation with a cross-country fundraiser on Harleys. Once again Oma would ride her own bike to Wisconsin and back stopping at various towns along the way to raise funds at pre-venued VFW's and Harley shops to raise both awareness and funds. I think we raised around $35,000 on that trip. One of our stops was the Air Force

*Academy where they were presenting life size memorial cases for your Dad and Jeremy Fresques. You were there with your Mom and soon to be, "Daddy Todd" who was one of the main speakers. Many Combat Controllers flew out to join us for the event.*

*On our trip back home we stayed in Williams Arizona with our next stop meeting up with Marine Corp Motorcycle Club at the Nevada border. While waiting for them I had received a message from your Uncle Jeff who knew our next stop was in Nevada. The message was strange as all he said was, "23 red, 23 red." So while we were waiting for the marines to show up I went into the casino and put $1.00 down on 23 red on the roulette table. I was the only one at the table so the dealer rolled the wheel asking me why I had picked 23 red. I shared with him that 23 was your dad's squadron and red represented his beret. Bing bing bing went the ball to roll right into the 23 red solt. I hit the mother lode at 35-5 odds. Opa has never really been a gambler but was more than happy to have won that very special $35.00. The dealer went on to tell me he raised, trained and supplied the Air Force Academy with falcons making the stop even more special. Truly I do believe your Dad was our guardian angel on that trip as against all odds Oma and Opa made it home safely without incident even though there were a few close calls.*

*Logan, I could go on and on about the brief time I knew your father Derek and it all boils down to his being an exceptional human being, son, husband, father, brother and uncle. He was such a great friend to so many. With Love, Opa March 2012*

I decided to bring these two letters into the same chapter as they represent two outstanding men in our lives. The paths in our lives bring exceptional miracles, and exceptional people. One of those men is my husband Todd, (Opa), and the other is my son-in-law, Todd.

*Dear Logan,*

*I can still remember in processing into the US Air Force Academy Prep School. It was the summer, and in Colorado, summers are hot and dry. I approached the small tent to register my name and around it formed a temporary line with yellow caution tape. There were several people at this tent, all of them official looking, even a chaplain whom I remember vividly telling me and my Mom and Dad that once you cross the line you can't come back. And this is where the journey begins.*

*Prep school was only a year long, but it was grueling. There were three squadrons, A, B, and C each with about 75 cadet candidates, or "preppies" as we were called. Since we endured a lot of challenges throughout that year and the fact that we were such a small number, we all grew to know each other and became very close. This is where I met your Dad, Derek. He wasn't hard to pick out since he was one of the tallest guys in the Prep School and he was one of the athletes. All of the athletes tended to group together whether they played football, baseball, tennis, or water polo like your Dad. Since I had come to the Air Force Academy to play football, I ran in the same circles with your Dad. Unfortunately, we weren't in the same squadron at Prep School. He was in A and I in B, so we never had the chance to form a strong friendship, but we always seemed to give each other the "what's up" nod in passing; a nod of respect from one athlete to another and a nod of friend to friend, even if more of by sharing the same circumstance of being at the Prep School. The best stories I know of your Dad at the Prep School were always of him being a bit of a jokester, being severely intense in whatever he did, and overall, just being known as a standup kind of guy. One memory I have is one of the heavier snows we had in Colorado in late 1996/early 1997. It was a free for all snowball fight against each squadron fiercely defending our own* teams in the snow. I remember your Dad, absolutely covered in snow, head to toe, running through B-squadron's defenses and throwing as many snow balls as possible. Of course, at that point, the snowball fight turned into a big wrestling match in the snow and he more or less started it. What I remember most from that was your Dad, fearless to charge and he was a leader.

Your Dad and I kept a similar relationship all throughout the four years at the Academy. Always a respect for one another but with different schedules, squadrons, and sports, we never really got to know each other. When I did hear about your Dad I heard nothing but great things and never in a way that I could ever think negatively of him.

My junior and senior year at the Air Force Academy I got to know another very special person. I had the privilege of meeting Jeremy Fresques. You've always known him as "Mr. Jeremy," and as my friend. Jeremy and I got to know each other over the last couple of years at the Academy. He was by all measures insanely into a fitness goal to ultimately reach his goal of becoming a member of the US Special Forces team. At that time I knew little about what that meant. I remember our junior to senior summer where Jeremy attended Mini-BUDS. I got to know how this is a pre-selector into one of the world's most elite fighting force; the Navy SEALS. The story I heard was how grueling it was and how Jeremy, and your Dad both went through it and did exceptionally well. These are the memories I have of your Dad at the time even though I still knew him only through brief interactions, stories, and because we were both "preppies." Jeremy spoke of Derek's tenacity and perseverance as remarkable and how the small group of the cadets that attended did overall very well through the program. I got a chance to peek into the mind of what that training regiment meant my senior year since Jeremy and I became roommates and workout buddies.

*We would wake up to the sound of his alarm clock radio at 5:30 am. I remember that for about four months straight from about September to December we woke up and made our way down to the gym before most cadets were up. I remember what it meant to have the mindset to continue to prepare to be a member of the elite team that Jeremy (and Derek) was preparing for. While I enjoyed the camaraderie, the early mornings and workouts that happened rain or shine (or heavy Colorado snow) were exhausting. Through my senior year I recall just how much loyalty and accountability I had from my roommate and friend. Jeremy was more disciplined and mentally tough that anyone I'd ever seen and I knew that once his alarm clock went off meant that we were getting up and facing a tough workout. Seeing this and experiencing it firsthand from Jeremy, meant that I knew your Dad was of the same caliber and was just as tough.*

*This was a period in my life where I had made a commitment to follow Jesus. I had struggled doing things "my way" and a series of events led me on my knees and He was seeking me. During this period when I accepted Him into my life I experienced things I never thought would happen. To be brief, after I had accepted Jesus into my heart on December 10, 1999 I not only tried to be the best example to Jeremy as I could, but I also shared with him what I had experienced. Through the months we trained and all through the first semester of our senior year I got to see Jeremy get more and more inquisitive, until on December 10, 2000, Jeremy stepped forward at the little Baptist church I invited him to and accepted the same gift I did a year prior. Seeing this happen on the very same day I did a year previous showed me that life isn't mere consequence, but divine plan from a creator bigger than my imagination.*

*I would be remiss talking about your Dad and how I came into your life had I not discussed this divine plan and how from the beginning God has ALWAYS ( and will always) have a plan.*

*After graduation every one of my classmates got their assignments and locations and all 846 of us went our separate ways. I had heard your Dad got his dream job of Special Forces and Jeremy and I kept in contact. Jeremy, due to headaches he had when he was a freshman was disqualified to join your Dad in the Special Forces pipeline. At that time, not knowing what else to do, he selected Communications, like I did. After only several months going through communications training, Jeremy re-applied and was selected to train in the Combat Control pipeline, just like your Dad. His dream was now being realized.*

*Jeremy and I continued to stay in close contact while I was living in Germany at my first assignment. I got a call from him one day while he was in the pipeline, and he asked if I wouldn't mind being his best man at his wedding in March of 2004. Of course I attended and got to meet his lovely bride, Lindsey for the first time. It was a beautiful wedding and the weather was absolutely breathtaking that weekend in Florida. That was not only my first trip to the Florida Gulf Coast, but also meeting Lindsey. While this was my first trip there, it was not going to be my last.*

*During the next year I moved to Tucson and attended two one and a half month long training sessions at Hurlburt Field in the spring of 2005. On the first training sessions I got to meet up with Lindsey and her sister Becky and got to get to know them better, and really enjoyed the beautiful weather and everything that makes that area of the US so wonderful. Following that six weeks, I went back to Tucson for a couple of weeks before my second training session began. I remember I was driving to my house on Memorial Day when I got a call from Lindsey. Lindsey told me that Jeremy was killed in a plane crash in Iraq. I later learned that several others were involved, including your Dad. This was the call that changed everything.*

*I found myself flying back early to Florida to meet with Lindsey and all of her family. There were lots of tears, some laughter as we shared memories, and lots of commotion. I also remember meeting you and your Mom the first time. We were in the 23$^{rd}$ CCT squadron at Hurlburt and I remember looking over at a young 10 month old white haired, blue eyed baby boy with such sadness because of the news. I also remember glancing over at your Mom and seeing her blue eyes through her red and sleep deprived sadness. This is a time I'll never forget.*

*Over the next couple of years I continued to keep in contact with Lindsey. I had transitioned out of the military into a civilian job and had moved from Arizona to Minnesota. During this time I routinely thought of my friends and classmates in that accident, the blonde haired blue eyed boy I saw at the memorial, and your Mom and the new life she was experiencing, even though none of us ever really met during that sad time.*

*In a series of events that only God can orchestrate, you and your Mom came rushing into my life. In the winter of 2007 I found myself booking airfare to Florida (once again) to officially meet that blond haired kid and his Mom. Leading up to December, your Mom and I talked multiple times throughout the day and continued to try to make sense of how and why we would meet. "Why me" I would ask, and then I remembered God's divine plan. It's this divine plan that kept me awake at night thinking of everything that was happening during this time in our lives and how we were being pulled together in a way that wasn't exactly our choice. Furthermore, during this humbling time, it brought forth the full emotions of that phone call and time of sadness in 2005 and brought full-circle the impact of what was going on and the responsibility that I faced. I recall thinking how big my responsibility would be to be in your life and how to best honor your Dad (and Jeremy) through knowing you and your Mom.*

*Over the course of six months, I left my job at the time in Minnesota and accepted a position in New Orleans. During this time I commuted every weekend to Florida for the better part of a year to spend every weekend with you and your Mom. I accepted the responsibility and the pleasure of loving you both unconditionally and the gift that God had placed in my life. I see why that sad time in 2005 stuck with me and how I could honor my friends and classmates by honoring those left behind.*

*In late 2008, with your help, I asked your Mom to marry me and in the Spring of 2009 we would be a family.*

*There is a lot to this story that I could go into with greater detail. These past handful of years have been the most rewarding, most challenging, and most monumental times in my life. I've gone from a single guy to a family man. By accepting God's amazing plan I've been granted the privilege of watching you grow into a fine young man and honoring your Dad by not only promising to protect you and your Mom, but also raise you respectfully in how I believe he would want me to raise you. In addition to the blessing of you being my son we now have two other children; a daughter and a son. So now you're a big, big brother and a fine one at that!*

*As I reflect on the sadness and tears and emptiness, I'm reminded that this life is short. I'm also constantly reminded that what we see is truly only temporary and the real gift, oftentimes is in the wake after the sadness. As evident of how two unlikely souls could meet, find love, and build a thriving family on the foundation of such sad events. My life story is not what I do for a living, what I have, or what clothes I wear, but what legacy I leave for my children. I believe in the power of parenthood and the unexpected blessings in life. For who are we to know and plan out our own blessings, when we have a creator that knows more about us than we do? I reflect on the impact of such sad events and how so much happiness has resulted. While this may sound trite or downplay Memorial Day 2005, I believe this happiness serves to highlight the purpose that these men continue to serve in all our hearts and know that their memories are shared often.*

*"Now faith is being sure of what we hope for and certain of what we do not see." Hebrew 11:1*

*With all my love from your Dad, Todd April 2012*

# Ten

On May 11, 2012, I was asked to attend a special ceremony at the Cabrillo High School swimming pool. There is a plaque on the wall of the pool enclosure that is dedicated to Derek. The family of a young man I had never met, called and asked if I would join them for the ceremony. When Mr. Andrews called to say that his son would like me to be there, he related a story that sounded very familiar. The story was about a young man that attended Cabrillo, played water polo, and tried to get an appointment to the Air Force Academy. His scores were not high enough, so he followed the path that Derek took. It is fitting that I share the last letter that I received as the last letter in this book.

*Dear Argel Family,*

*I need and want to share with you my thoughts and feelings about your son Derek as a result of my readings about his life. First and foremost I want to say thank you. Thank you for your son's life and the contribution that he made in keeping this great nation of ours safe. I feel a connection with Derek. I am a four-year Cabrillo aquatics athlete who applied for entry into the Air Force Academy beginning last summer. Although I made a number of critical cuts during the selection process, I received notification that I was not selected for the appointment. That said, in reading about Derek and the prep school I was encouraged to continue my quest for an appointment. I realized through Derek's example of steadfast determination, dedication, perseverance, and an appreciation for hard work that any obstacle can be overcome. Today I can say that I am a Northwestern Prep graduate with an appointment to attend the US Air Force Academy class of 2016.*

*Derek's life has become an example to me about what is good and decent in the human nature of man. Frankly, it wasn't one particular story about Derek but the culmination effect of all those examples of what defined Derek's character. For me Derek's strongest character traits were his absolute honesty, sense of decency and fairness, unwavering commitment to excellence in everything he did, and his strong sense of loyalty to family, friends and teammates. Those are the characteristics I know you cherish. Those are also the character traits I am learning and want to live by.*

*Although I want very much to succeed in everything I do in life, as demonstrated by Derek, I want to succeed in the light of humbleness and the recognition that regardless of the career path I choose, I will seek and reserve some part of my life in the service of others. That service may be to my country, community, or another venue that serves our fellow man. I also understand there will be situations in my life which present difficulties, disappointments, adversity, and challenges. My desire and hope is that like Derek, my decisions concerning those difficult times are based on a core set of values that I have established and worked to exercise in all that I do.*

*Now with a strong value system in tow, my positive life experiences, and examples like Derek Argel, I will soon begin to pursue my dreams and take my first step on to the pathway connecting the young man I am today with the successful person I hope to become. At nineteen years old, I am equipped and anxious to grow as a person and face the next challenge in my life, and I am well prepared. My eyes are wide open towards my rapidly approaching future, and I stand eagerly at the horizon.*

*Again, I thank you from the bottom of my heart for your son Derek's life. May God comfort and bless you in the knowledge that the character of Derek's life is still bearing fruit today.*

*Sincerely, Keenan Andrews May, 2012*

What a tremendous gift Keenan's letter was to us, and what a blessing to receive it before this book was published.

*Dear Grandson,*

*There really is no conclusion to this story. It is now exactly seven years to the day that we received the information. So much has happened and our lives have changed radically. I remind people that talk to me about closure, that there really is no such thing. Pain and sorrow are part of everyone's life. We learn to walk with it. We learn that we can make a difference in other's lives through our loss. The impact that our loved ones had on us and others is something that can be cherished the rest of our lives. It was and is their gift to us.*

*There were some exceptional men on the plane with your Dad that day. Major William "Brian" Downs was the pilot. He graduated from Westminster Christian Academy in Saint Louis, Missouri in 1983, and from Grove City College, Pennsylvania, with a degree in international business. He was commissioned in the US Air Force in February 1988. Following Undergraduate Pilot Training graduation in April 1989 from Columbus Air Force Base, Mississippi, Major Downs attended B-52 Combat*

*Crew Training School at Castle Air Force Base, California. In December 1992, Major Downs joined the 9th Special Operations Squadron, 1st Special Operations Wing, Hurlburt Field, Florida, as a MC-130P Combat Shadow pilot. In September 1997, Major Downs was assigned to the 6th Special Operations Squadron, Hurlburt Field, Florida, where after two tours, he became one of the best Combat Aviation Advisors in the unit's history. Major Downs separated from active duty Air Force in December 1999. After the September 11th terrorist attacks, Major Downs returned to active duty with the Air Commandos of the 6th Special Operations Squadron.*

*Captain Jeremy J. Fresques was a native of Farmington, New Mexico. He entered the Air Force in May of 2001 after completing four years at the USAF Academy in Colorado Springs. Before entering the Special Tactics community, Captain Fresques served as a Flight Commander at the 56th Communications Squadron at Luke Air Force Base, Arizona. In 2002, after successfully completing Special Tactics Officer Selection, and training, Captain Fresques was assigned to the 23rd STS at Hurlburt Field, Florida where he served as the Assistant Team Leader for Silver Team.*

*Staff Sergeant Casey Crate was born in Spanaway, Washington. After graduating from Spanaway Lake High School in 1996, he enlisted in the Air Force and entered active duty on 1 July, 1998. He attended Basic Training at Lackland Air Force Base. Following Basic Training and tech school, he was assigned to the 16th Aircraft Maintenance Squadron at Hurlburt Field, Florida. In June of 2002, he entered the Special Tactics pipeline to become an Air Force Combat Controller. Following graduation he was assigned to Silver Team at the 23rd Special Tactics Squadron at Hurlburt Field.*

*Capt. Ali Abass served with the Iraqi Air Force. He was hailed a hero by the American Forces for actions he performed on one mission where he saved the life of an American Colonel. He worked closely with the Americans. I remain close to his widow and have had the opportunity to spend time with her in Washington DC during two of her visits here.*

*I have intentionally left out the collective medals, achievement awards, and decorations each of these men were awarded. None of them would want that to be a focal point of their lives. The Combat Control Airmen are called "The Quiet Professionals." For this reason, the world will not know of their accomplishments, constant deployments and work they do worldwide. Their motto is simply, "First There, That Others May Live."*

*Your Dad and Jeremy pinned on the rank of Captain that morning. You could have told them both that they were pinning on the rank of General and it would not have deterred them from the focus of their mission.*

*There was some humor as usual that morning. Of course, there was another uniform issue with Derek. He forgot his camouflage pants back at his base. Casey had a wonderful sense of humor and offered to loan Derek some of his. Casey was much shorter than your Dad, but Derek put the pants on anyway. When he came out in front of everyone, the pants came just below his knees. He posed for them, did a little dance, let everyone have a good laugh, then made the decision that they would go in civilian clothes. This is not unusual for the Special Ops guys to wear civilian clothing in the field. They had breakfast with their friends, shared more jokes and laughs and boarded the plane. They shook hands with the folks on the ground and in great spirits, with much excitement about the mission, took off into a beautiful sky.*

*The Airmen on that plane on Memorial Day of 2005 were bound to each other in the brotherhood of an elite Special Forces Unit. They were also bound together by something much stronger and that was their faith. Of all of the collective training, the tools in their belts, the combined knowledge of their years, the most powerful tool they carried was their faith in God. They knew that God has a plan for each of us, and that we don't question that plan. Your Dad knew and said that God would call for him when he was ready.*

*I mentioned at the beginning of this book that some people say they can count their friends on one hand in their adult lives, but that your Dad was an exception to that rule. His faith, his countless friends and you were his greatest blessings. In everything, he thanked God for the opportunities he had, and prayed for the strength to accomplish his goals to be of service to others.*

*On May 30, 2005, I couldn't feel the sun anymore. I walked in darkness for a very long time. It wasn't a matter of losing faith, but losing my direction. Some people wanted me to be "back to normal", but had no idea what normal was for me now. This new journey is for the rest of my life. Opa and I were very fortunate to find a wonderful way to help other children. It is the organization your Dad used to help. We were not only helping the children, but by doing so we were helping ourselves too. We started to see some light through the darkness. The light slowly became brighter. I think God provided a path of light for us to walk on. We just had to stay on that path and in the light.*

*If we walk with faith, we know that blessings can be born out of terrible tragedies. This takes time. It may be hard for some to understand that when I talk about our family, I talk about how very blessed we are. We have had nothing short of miracles in our lives.*

*Your Dad (Todd) wrote about how he came into our lives. Since I don't believe in coincidence or accidents, but only in God's plan, our paths did not cross by mistake. So many things happened early on. The first time I remember seeing him was at the graduation ceremony from the Air Force Prep School. I don't see very well at a distance, so while they were on the parade field I kept pointing to Todd and saying "Hey, that's Derek!" Both of them were about the same height. Everyone kept correcting me. I did it again when I was watching the video when we got home. I had a funny feeling and wondered who the other tall man was. We would meet again in Colorado Springs for the dedication of Derek and Jeremy's Memorial cases at the Academy. I really got to know him then and really grew to love him as a person. He delivered such a wonderful talk about Jeremy and their friendship. He had a wonderful sense of humor and a great personality. When I visited you and your Mom in Florida, Todd came to visit from New Orleans. He told me a great story. It seemed he had a graduation picture in his office of the entire graduating class of 2001 from the Air Force Academy. He and your Mom looked everywhere in the photo for your Dad. They did this several times but could not find him. They looked for him with his usual group of friends, or with the water polo guys. They still could not find him. Finally one day, they found him. He was standing directly behind your Dad Todd. This brought such a comforting feeling over me. They stood together, just as our family stands together today.*

*We are so blessed that such a wonderful man came into our lives. We are blessed that you now have a little sister and brother to love, and that your mother has found the happiness and love that she deserves.*

*Your Daddy Derek would have wanted all of this for you. I'm sure he is looking down on all of us from heaven with that wonderful grin, knowing that God has a plan for all of us.*

*In the past seven years we have forged ahead with new friendships, old friendships and our growing family. We have had the opportunity to speak about our family as well as learn from so many others. Although we miss Derek each and every day of our lives, we are comforted to know that in his 28 years on this earth he made such a lasting impression. Through the stories and letters that continue to come in, he is still making a difference.*

*With all of my love, Oma May 30, 2012*

Made in the USA
Coppell, TX
28 December 2019